GW01396307

salades

Acclaimed chef Damien Pignolet shows us the endless possibilities of the salad. Here are entrée salads to stimulate the appetite, side salads to refresh the palate, and warm salads that serve as a meal in their own right. Learn how to perfect classic salads, such as niçoise, and how to marry a range of tastes and textures to create a chicken salad with asparagus, peaches and a pistachio nut vinaigrette, and a sweet salad of strawberry, orange and red wine.

Damien's first book, *French*, captured the essence of classic French cooking in Australia. With its rich photography and detailed notes on produce, composition and presentation, *Salades* is set to educate, inspire and delight the dedicated home cook.

DAMIEN PIGNOLET is generally recognised as one of Australia's finest chefs and restaurateurs. As chef and co-owner of Sydney restaurants such as Claude's from 1981 to 1993 and Bistro Moncur from 1993 onwards, his eye for detail and his consummate French style have garnered him many accolades. He has also been an influential teacher of cookery for more than three decades. In 2004 he became executive chef and co-proprietor of the Bellevue Hotel and Dining Room, also in Sydney. His highly regarded, award-winning first book, *French*, was published in 2005.

To Mogens Bay Esbensen,
my mentor

salades

Damien Pignolet

with photography by Anson Smart

LANTERN
an imprint of
PENGUIN BOOKS

Contents

Introduction

The role of salads in the French kitchen is quite different from what one might expect in Australian and British cooking, where a bowl of green leaves is usually what passes under this title. The Americans have the closest connection to the French concept by beginning a meal with a salad drawn from a wide repertoire.

The word 'salad' comes from an Old Provençal word *salada*, which has its origins in the Latin *sal*, meaning 'salt'. The aim of this book is to open our mind to the vast possibilities available within this genre. The idea of confining salads to a mixture of lettuce leaves, sliced beetroot and tomatoes served with the main course will be dispelled as I explore seasonal raw materials and their marriage with classic and modern dressings.

The French use the generic term *salade composée* – composed salad – to distinguish between a simple green leaf salad following the main course and one that holds its own place within a meal, served generally at the beginning of a structured menu. The purpose of a *salade composée* should be to offer a gentle start to a meal and is often driven by the combination of fresh flavours and textures to stimulate the palate in preparation for the more substantial dishes to follow.

I have also provided a chapter of recipes for salads that are satisfying enough to serve as a main course in their own right [see pages 77 to 103], and a chapter of salads that are best served as an accompaniment to another

dish [see pages 105 to 133]. The French also like to serve warm salads [see pages 151 to 165], one of the ongoing legacies of Nouvelle Cuisine. There is also a chapter on winter salads, as the French do not regard salad as only the preserve of summer [see pages 167 to 191]. To finish off, there is a chapter on sweet salads [see pages 193 to 209] based on seasonal fruits that make a delightful ending for a well-constructed menu.

Composing any dish and, for that matter, any creation within the arts, calls for a clear understanding of what constitutes balance. In classical music, composition of the movements of a concerto or string quartet might offer a range of tempi such as slow, fast and moderate, to bring the work into both intellectual and emotional equilibrium. Similarly, the instruments employed by a cook in creating a dish are the chosen raw materials woven into balance as governed by our sense of taste. Balancing salt, acid, bitter and sour, and sweet will ensure a satisfying dish, provided that due consideration is given to the textures of the ingredients used. Sometimes a different texture can provide an element of contrast, such as the crunchy croûtons and crisp cos lettuce leaves in a Caesar salad. A thorough understanding of the nature of the chosen raw materials will guide you towards a structured and satisfying salad.

Much of what we enjoy about any dish is governed by our initial response to its visual presentation. Although the contrasting colours and three-dimensional structure of a salad's ingredients will generally excite the palate, never let visual considerations overrule the importance of flavour. The successful composition of any dish is only as good as the balance created by it tasting delicious. So start by imagining how a salad will taste by putting the prime raw material at the top of the list, then selecting others that will offer a contrast by way of flavour and texture. Finally, consider what elements the dressing needs to marry all the ingredients and a balance should emerge.

So now that a salad has been created, what about the wine? Over some thirty years of working with young chefs in the nine restaurants I have created, I frequently need to remind them of the role played by wine in the enjoyment of a dish. For example, a very simple salad of great-tasting tomatoes, olives, mozzarella and bitter leaves with balsamic vinaigrette may destroy a wine if the olives are really acidic. Taste the raw materials, then taste the vinaigrette, and then taste the wine and a better understanding will emerge. Consider the weight, if you like, of the flavours and how they will mount on the palate as the salad is eaten when selecting the vinaigrette and the wine. Matching any dish with

an appropriate wine is an exciting challenge and only experience will help the cook to master balance; but what fun!

Although there have been many books written on the subject of salads, my objective in writing this book is to introduce you to the broader domain of salads, especially those in the French tradition of composed salads, but also the vast repertoire of salads served as an entrée or accompaniment to a main course, or as a main course in their own right.

The challenge for all cooks is to create a dish where the balance of flavour, texture and visual presentation are harmonious. I hope that this book will guide you to this reward.

In the recipes, * indicates an ingredient, technique or piece of equipment that is explained more fully in the Glossary [see pages 210 to 216] or for which suppliers are given in the Suppliers section [see pages 217 to 218].

Lettuces & Other Salad Leaves

Arugula

See 'Rocket [Arugula]'.

Beetroot Greens or Leaves

Only the smallest leaves are suitable to include in a salad since the larger leaves are too tough.

Belgian Endive

See 'Witlof [Belgian Endive]'.

Butter Lettuce (1)

The pale green soft leaves are loose and delicate in texture and flavour. Ideal to mix with a bitter, firm-textured leaf such radicchio, moistened with a rich vinaigrette based on blue cheese or fresh goat's cheese.

Cabbage

Choose only the youngest cabbages, and use finely shredded in salads. The Savoy variety is lovely very finely shredded, seasoned with salt and freshly ground white pepper, then moistened with extra virgin olive oil and a well-aged balsamic vinegar; Fratelli Fresh's restaurant Sopra in Macleay Street, Potts Point, Sydney, makes a splendid version of this salad.

Celery Leaves (2)

The pale inner leaves of celery have a deliciously bitter, refreshing taste with a peppery finish; they add a zing to a salad of blander leaves. Deep-fry celery leaves to finish a salad of firm tomatoes* such as Love Bite or a mixture of cherry, teardrop and small truss tomatoes, dressed with extra virgin olive oil and a touch of excellent white-wine vinegar. The tomatoes will benefit from being lightly salted and drained for 15 minutes, then patted dry.

Chicory (3)

The long stems should be discarded and the leaves torn into small pieces. Chicory is rather bitter and is best used in small quantities along with leaves such as those of cos and red oak lettuce. Dress with a garlic and mustard vinaigrette bound with coddled egg yolks.

For a warm salad, wilt chicory in a covered pan with a little water over low heat, then drain and combine it with warm caramelised onion and crisply fried croûtons and dress with a walnut oil vinaigrette. See also 'Radicchio [Red & Treviso]'.

Corn Salad

See 'Mâche'.

Cos Lettuce (4)

The leaves are crisp with a very slightly bitter, fresh flavour. Also known as romaine lettuce in the United States, its texture lends itself to rich dressings and it is the correct leaf to use in a Caesar salad. The stability of the leaves makes them excellent for salads destined to be eaten with the hands, as is the original method for enjoying a Caesar salad, since they are firm enough to support other ingredients. A fresh herb mayonnaise is the perfect accompaniment for cos leaves.

Dandelion Leaves [Baby] (5)

Dandelion leaves are extremely bitter and most of the stems should be discarded. Use in a salad of sweeter crisp leaves such as baby cos to provide a balance of flavour. Excellent with soft poached eggs, fried walnuts and crisp garlic croûtons dressed with walnut oil vinaigrette.

Endive

See 'Frisée [Curly-leaf Endive]', 'Witlof [Belgian Endive]'.

Frisée [Curly-leaf Endive] (6)

Frisée is one of the most frequently used lettuces in France and features as Salade Frisée Lardons [see page 54] on bistro and brasserie menus all over the country. It has firm curly leaves and a delicate, bitter taste that is well suited for matching with soft poached eggs, richly flavoured fried bacon and walnuts.

Frisée in Australia is very large and the outer leaves are dark green and very bitter, making them suitable only for cooking. However, the inner leaves are white to pale green and are perfect for the salads in this book. Take care to check the root ends of curly endive washed ahead of use since they tend to discolour and should be trimmed off.

1

2

3

4

5

6

7

8

9

10

11

12

Iceberg Lettuce (7)

Just about the only lettuce commercially grown in Australia until the early 1970s, this tightly packed, pale-green lettuce has a wonderful crispness and clean flavour, despite many considering it dull. I like to include some chunks of iceberg with softer and spicy leaves for the balance its crispness brings to a salad. The English use a cooked cream dressing spiced with dry mustard and a touch of cayenne pepper to moisten shredded iceberg.

Lamb's Lettuce

See 'Mâche'.

Lettuce

See 'Butter Lettuce', 'Cos Lettuce', 'Iceberg Lettuce', 'Mignonette Lettuce', 'Oak-leaf Lettuce'.

Mâche [Lamb's Lettuce or Corn Salad] (8)

Naturally grown mâche leaves should be about 5cm long and are wider at the tip. The leaves are prized in France for their slightly nutty, sweet flavour and delicate texture, as well as their appearance.

Until recently, only very small punnets were available in Australia and, more to the point, they had little to do with the natural product since they were cultivated hydroponically. However, Frais Farms in Victoria now offer 'mâche rosettes' in 100g packs that have an excellent flavour and appearance.

Mesclun (9)

The true mesclun [origin South of France, known as *mesclumo*] is a melange of leaves from wild plants, including baby mizuna, rocket, mâche, purslane and chervil; it may also contain some oak leaf lettuce. While the wild varieties may be hard to find, one can assemble a decent mesclun salad using a combination of these leaves. Dress with extra virgin olive oil or a mixture of walnut and vegetable oil and a good-quality red-wine vinegar such as Forum Cabernet vinegar* in a bowl seasoned with bruised garlic.

Mignonette Lettuce

This gently flavoured lettuce has soft, dark green leaves beautifully tinged with red tips. It is a relative of the butter lettuce but has finer textured leaves. Serve with a simple garlic-infused extra virgin olive oil vinaigrette or as part of a mesclun mixture.

Miner's Lettuce

See 'Purslane'.

Mizuna (10)

The dark green leaves are feathery in texture with a delicate, mustardy, slightly acidic flavour. Dress with one part light sesame oil and five parts vegetable oil vinaigrette with a touch of lime juice.

Mustard Greens

These little leaves come in a wide variety of shapes, colours and sizes. All have a distinctive mustardy character that adds an element of spice to a salad of milder flavoured leaves.

Nasturtium Leaves & Flowers (11)

Baby nasturtium leaves have a hot, spicy flavour and make a good addition to a mesclun mixture. The flowers are yellow and very pretty in appearance and edible if unsprayed. Serve both in a mixed salad with fried garlic croûtons as a refreshing starter or with snow pea shoots to accompany a country terrine.

Oak-leaf Lettuce (12)

The heads have loosely packed, curly leaves and a mild but distinctive taste. The colours vary within both the green and red varieties. Combine with spicy leaves such as rocket and nasturtium and a crunchy leaf such as baby cos for an elegant-looking bowl of greens.

Purslane [Miner's lettuce]

The dull green leaves of this plant are flat and fleshy with moist, edible stems. They have an elongated ovular shape with a lemony, tart flavour; some say it is akin to that of baby sorrel leaves. Purslane adds freshness and a juicy firm texture to a leaf salad. It marries well with tomatoes, beetroot, spring onions, mild white salad onions and herbs such as parsley, mint and dill. Add purslane leaves to a salad of purple and golden baby beetroot with finely sliced spring onions and dress with tarragon vinaigrette.

Radicchio [Red & Treviso] (13)

These are members of the chicory family and share varying degrees of bitterness, from bittersweet to very bitter flavours. I have not come across the pink-tinged Castelfranco variety in this country but it is considered the mildest in flavour with tender leaves. Treviso is quite bitter with elongated leaves, in contrast to the bulb shape of the red variety. The latter has tightly packed, firm-textured leaves and should be torn or sliced into small pieces for salads. The inherent bitterness is a good match for the salty flavour of goat's and blue cheeses. Ribbons of radicchio and chunks of tomato, dressed with a mild garlic vinaigrette or just extra virgin olive oil and balsamic vinegar, make a great salad for barbecued meat and game such as butterflied quail.

Rocket [Arugula] (14)

There are many varieties of this popular salad plant, all offering varying degrees of spicy, peppery flavour. In my opinion, the overuse of this flavourful leaf in every café and restaurant has taken away much of its charm. I guess it has replaced the humble parsley sprigs that adorned almost every dish for countless years.

I love really fresh, wild rocket [although it is now grown commercially] with its unruly shaped dark-green leaves and a super hit of spiciness. The simplest salad of full-flavoured tomatoes and wild rocket dressed with extra virgin olive oil and aged balsamic vinegar is always a treat. Rocket marries well with beetroot, parmesan and goat's cheese to name a few combinations.

Snow Pea Shoots (15)

Green pea, sugar snap and snow pea shoots add freshness and texture to a bowl of salad leaves. They are great in a chicken and mayonnaise sandwich or a beetroot and fresh goat's cheese salad. Sauté snow pea shoots over high heat in very little vegetable oil, then add to a bunch of sliced red radishes and toasted sesame seeds or toasted slivered almonds for a delicious warm salad.

Sorrel

Baby sorrel leaves have a lovely, fresh lemony tang that livens up a salad of crisp cos leaves mixed with the slightly bitter tips of witlof. Rub a bowl with a smashed clove of garlic, discard the debris, then make a vinaigrette consisting of one part walnut oil, one part vegetable oil and one part crème fraîche, then season lightly and acidulate with a little cider vinegar. Larger leaves should have their very bitter stems removed then cut into a chiffonnade [very fine strips].

Spinach [Baby] (16)

Baby spinach will add some gentle acidity to a green leaf salad. Use a good handful or two in a leaf salad for four people and dress with a simple vinaigrette or the walnut oil, vegetable oil and crème fraîche dressing above. I have called for baby spinach in many of the composed salads in this book [see pages 1 to 51] as it is readily available and easy to prepare.

Larger leaves call for the removal of their tough stems, then being torn into manageable pieces. Chopped hard-boiled eggs, fried croûtons and finely grated parmesan cheese partner well with the higher level of acidity found in mature spinach leaves.

Watercress

One of my favourite greens; I love its spiciness, colour and appearance. Any green salad will benefit from the addition of watercress. Avoid the coarse main stalks by plucking little sprigs from them.

Witlof [Belgian Endive] (17)

The pale green leaves are tightly packed within the long heads. The leaves blend very well with seared scallops, fresh and hard goat's cheeses, Roquefort cheese, poached chicken and seared chicken livers. The texture is delicately crisp and the flavour refreshingly bitter. There is also a red variety. Never wash witlof since the leaves loose their crispness immediately – simply wipe any dirt away with a moistened paper towel. Hazelnut and walnut oils are a perfect match for witlof.

13

14

15

16

17

Composed Salads

Salades composées

12–18 baby beetroot, scrubbed

1 small cauliflower, cut into small florets*

18–24 cherry tomatoes, halved lengthwise

1 small clove garlic, lightly smashed

2 teaspoons thyme leaves

60ml extra virgin olive oil

sea salt and freshly ground black pepper

a splash aged red-wine vinegar [such as
Forum Cabernet vinegar*]

1 head each red and white witlof [or 2 white witlof],
outer leaves discarded

3–4 tablespoons freshly grated horseradish,* or prepared
horseradish,* to taste

125ml crème fraîche*

1 teaspoon lemon juice

a little cold water, to thin the dressing

½ celeriac, peeled and cut into 3mm julienne strips

1 bunch chives, finely chopped [optional]

Serves 6

Cauliflower, Beetroot & Celeriac Salad with Horseradish Cream

This is a great entrée for the winter months when celeriac and fresh horseradish* are available. A good-quality purchased horseradish* such as Tracklements brand may be substituted, of course, if the task of grating horseradish is too daunting. That said, if you have a fruit juice extractor, simply peel the fresh horseradish and put it through the extractor, then mix the grated pulp with the collected juice. Season this with salt and a little lemon juice. Don't be concerned about the beetroot discolouring the cauliflower.

1 Preheat the oven to 160°C. Wrap each beetroot in foil and bake for 30 minutes, then test for tenderness with a fine skewer; the skewer should almost fall through the beetroot. This will ensure they are cooked and their sweetness is fully developed. Cool for 5 minutes, then squeeze the foil gently to release the skin from each beetroot.

2 Soak the cauliflower in very cold water for 10 minutes, then cook in boiling salted water for 2–3 minutes or until still slightly crisp. Drain and refresh under cold running water, then drain well. Turn onto a clean dry tea towel to absorb any remaining water.

3 Place the tomato, garlic, thyme leaves and olive oil in a small shallow pan and season lightly with salt and pepper. Place over the lowest possible heat and allow the tomato to soften so that a little juice merges with the oil. This may take up to 10 minutes. The idea is to perfume the oil and barely soften the tomato, thus releasing more flavour. Transfer to a deep wide plate to cool, adding a little splash of vinegar to the oil, then adjust the seasoning to taste.

4 Cut 3cm-long tips from the witlof and reserve, then slice the remainder thinly, avoiding the core.

5 Combine the horseradish, crème fraîche and lemon juice in a small bowl and season to taste, then, adding a teaspoon of water at a time, dilute to a thickish pouring consistency.

6 Toss the cauliflower, celeriac and witlof with just enough dressing to coat them lightly and share between 6 deep entrée plates. Distribute the beetroot equally [if some are larger, cut them to match the smaller ones], then lightly coat with the horseradish dressing. Tuck the witlof tips here and there between the vegetables.

7 Distribute the tomato over the salads, then moisten the tomato and beetroot with some of the tomato poaching oil. Scatter with the chives, if using, and serve immediately.

24 baby beetroot, scrubbed	
3 litres water	
sea salt	
1kg broad beans in pods, shelled	
½ large head celeriac	
juice of ½ lemon	
18 white pickling onions	
100g walnut kernels, each broken into 4–5 pieces	
2 teaspoons walnut oil	
1 handful frisée lettuce, or 1½ cups finely shaved iceberg lettuce, washed and spin-dried	

Walnut cream vinaigrette

1 small clove garlic, smashed
40ml walnut oil
40ml crème fraîche*
sea salt and freshly ground white pepper
about 20ml cider vinegar* or aged sherry vinegar
Serves 6

Broad Bean, Baby Beetroot, Celeriac & White Onion Salad with Walnut Cream Vinaigrette

This elegant salad calls for the tiniest beetroot you can find, preferably both golden and purple varieties. Generally small pickling onions are graded randomly, but again look for the smallest or cut the larger ones in half from the top to root end after they are cooked. The vinaigrette is unusual since it uses crème fraîche* as well as walnut oil. If using shaved iceberg it should be placed on the plates before the broad bean mixture. Very suitable to precede feathered game such as roast squab, quail or guinea fowl.

1 Trim the stalks about 2cm above the beetroot and wash if needed. Place in a large saucepan of cold salted water. Bring to the boil and simmer for 15–25 minutes until tender. Drain and slip off the skins and stalks while the beetroot are still warm.

2 Bring the water to the boil, then add 1 tablespoon salt and return to the boil. Add the broad beans and cook for 2 minutes. Check for tenderness by squeezing off the husk and tasting a bean. Drain and refresh under cold running water. Drain again, then gently squeeze to release the bright green beans from their greyish-green shells. This may be done in advance but be sure to dry and refrigerate them once they have been shelled.

3 Peel the celeriac and cut crosswise into 3mm-thick slices using a mandoline* or sharp knife. Cut the slices into julienne, toss in the lemon juice to prevent discolouration, then pour off the excess juice and pat dry with paper towel.

4 Trim the onions at the base, taking care to keep the root intact. Pierce each onion with a thin paring knife and put them into a pan of cold salted water. Bring to the boil and cook for 15 minutes or until tender. They should still be a little firm. Drain, refresh briefly under cold running water and drain again.

5 Toss the walnuts in the walnut oil to coat, then toast in a dry frying pan over low heat, keeping the pan moving and tossing the nuts about until they gain a little colour. Tip onto paper towel to drain and pat dry.

6 For the vinaigrette, rub a small bowl with the garlic and discard its debris. Whisk the oil, crème fraîche, salt, pepper and vinegar until well combined, then adjust the seasoning to taste.

7 Combine the broad beans, celeriac and walnuts in a bowl with a little of the vinaigrette, then toss and distribute between 6 entrée plates. Separately moisten the beetroot and onions with some vinaigrette and divide between each plate. Scatter with sprigs of frisée and finish with more vinaigrette if needed.

1 small cauliflower, cut into small florets*	60ml extra virgin olive oil
2 apples [such as Gala]	20ml vegetable oil
juice of ½ lemon	20ml walnut oil
2–3 pale inner stalks celery, cut into 3cm batons	20–30ml cider vinegar*
4 spring onions, including a little of the green tops, peeled and roots removed, finely sliced	1 bunch watercress, short sprigs only, washed and spin-dried
⅓ cup finely chopped curly-leaf parsley	about 1 teaspoon hot smoked paprika* [such as Spanish La Chinata brand]
4 eggs, at fridge temperature	2 handfuls rocket leaves, washed and spin-dried, any coarse stalks removed
1 teaspoon Dijon mustard	
sea salt and freshly ground white pepper	**Serves 6**

Raw Cauliflower Salad with Coddled Eggs & Watercress

A lovely entrée for the warmer months or to precede a rustic main course such as braised beef or lamb shanks. The soft texture of the eggs adds body to the somewhat bland flavour of the cauliflower, while the rocket adds a spicy tone.

1   Soak the cauliflower in very cold water for 10 minutes, then drain. Plunge into boiling salted water for 30 seconds only. Drain and refresh under cold running water then drain well. Turn onto a clean dry tea towel to absorb any remaining water.

2   Peel the apples, cut into quarters, remove the cores and slice thinly directly into a bowl with the lemon juice, then toss well. Drain and pat dry with paper towel.

3   Combine the well-drained cauliflower, apple, celery, spring onion and parsley in a large mixing bowl.

4   Prick the eggs with a pin at the widest end. Lower into a small saucepan of boiling water and retrieve 1 egg after 3 minutes but cook the remaining 3 for an additional 4 minutes. Refresh the 3 eggs under cold running water then shell them carefully by gently tapping the shell. Cut into quarters.

5   Crack the shell of the 3-minute egg in the centre and scoop out the contents into a small mixing bowl. Whisk in the mustard, ¼ teaspoon salt and some pepper, then whisk in the oils slowly as for a mayonnaise, acidulating with enough vinegar to provide a sharp finish. The apple is also acidulated so keep this in mind when adding the vinegar.

6   Pour the mayonnaise over the vegetables and toss gently, then distribute between 6 deep entrée plates. Decorate with the watercress and place 2 egg quarters on each salad, dust with the paprika, then scatter with the rocket and serve.

12–18 thin leeks, trimmed of all but a trace of the
green tops

sea salt

3 eggs, at fridge temperature

about ½ iceberg lettuce, core removed, washed and
spin-dried, finely shredded

½ cup finely chopped curly-leaf parsley

Vinaigrette

1 heaped teaspoon Dijon mustard

125ml extra virgin olive oil

30–40ml tarragon vinegar or white-wine vinegar

sea salt and freshly ground black pepper

Serves 6

Leeks Vinaigrette

My take on this classic dish is probably more of an hors
d'oeuvre than a salad, since the classic recipe consists
of poached leeks dressed with a French vinaigrette.
I like this variation as it offers a little crunch against
the soft texture of the leeks and is a really easy entrée
to prepare. Leeks vinaigrette also makes a lovely
accompaniment to poached salmon with anchovy
butter. Put a bowl of steamed kipfler or chat potatoes
on the table for guests to help themselves for a perfect
simple meal.

1 Make a 2–3cm incision in the centre of the trimmed
green tops of the leeks and place them, green-side
down, in cold water. Leave for 10 minutes so that
any dirt may be released. Trim off the roots, taking
care not to disturb the hard bottoms that hold the
leeks together.

2 Select a wide pan that will accommodate the leeks
in one layer [or cook them in two batches]. Place the
leeks in the pan and cover with cold water, adding salt
to taste. Be sure the leeks are completely submerged.
Bring to the boil over high heat, then cover with a piece
of baking paper and simmer gently for 10 minutes or
so until the leeks are tender but offer some resistance
when pierced with a knife tip. Drain and refresh under
cold running water, then stand them, green-side down,
in a colander to drain.

3 Meanwhile, prick the eggs with a pin then lower into
a saucepan of boiling water for 9 minutes. Drain and
refresh under cold running water then shell the eggs
and chop them coarsely.

4 To make the vinaigrette, place the mustard, olive oil
and 20ml of the vinegar in a screw-top jar with
a good pinch of salt and some pepper, then shake well.
Taste and adjust with extra vinegar, salt and pepper
to achieve a slightly acid finish.

5 Distribute the shaved iceberg between 6 entrée plates,
placing the leeks on top. Moisten with the vinaigrette,
then scatter with the egg and parsley and serve
immediately.

4 small heads broccoli, cut into small florets※

sea salt

⅓ cup blanched salted pistachio nut kernels

olive oil spray

20ml pistachio or almond oil

60ml olive oil

10–20ml best quality aged white-wine vinegar [preferably Forum Chardonnay vinegar※]

freshly ground white pepper

1 blood or navel orange

1 bulb baby fennel, outer ribs and stalks removed [retain the fronds if still attached]

2 inner leaves red radicchio, washed and spin-dried

6 outer leaves red radicchio, washed and spin-dried, to serve

Serves 6

Broccoli, Fennel & Orange Salad with Pistachio Nut Vinaigrette

The bitterness of the radicchio offers a contrast to the aromatic sweetness of the fennel and the acidity of the diced orange in this salad. The nutty flavour of pistachios blends so well with the broccoli. An excellent entrée for almost any menu. If pistachio or almond oil are not on hand simply replace both oils with extra virgin olive oil and increase the pistachio nuts by ¼ cup.

1 Blanch the broccoli in a saucepan of boiling salted water for 1–2 minutes after the water returns to the boil, keeping the broccoli still slightly crisp. Drain and refresh under cold running water, then drain again. Leave in a colander for 15 minutes or more so that the water can drain away thoroughly.

2 Meanwhile, spray the pistachios lightly with olive oil spray and toast in dry frying pan over low–medium heat until they attain a little colour, then tip onto a chopping board to cool. Set aside half the nuts for a garnish. Finely chop the remaining pistachios, then combine with the two oils, vinegar, salt and pepper for the vinaigrette.

3 For the orange, follow the technique for filleting citrus fruit,※ collecting any juice as you go. Cut each fillet into 3–4 pieces. Add 2 teaspoons of the collected orange juice to the pistachio vinaigrette, then check the seasoning again and, if required, adjust with more orange juice, salt and pepper.

4 Trim the fennel top and bottom, then cut lengthwise into quarters and shave very thinly using a mandoline.※ Moisten with a little vinaigrette, then add the orange.

5 Roll the inner radicchio leaves into cigar shapes and shave quite thinly with a sharp knife, then add to the fennel and orange fillets.

6 Distribute the fennel and orange mixture between the 6 outer radicchio leaves. Moisten the broccoli florets with enough vinaigrette to coat them lightly and present them on top of the salads.

7 Roughly chop the reserved pistachios and scatter over the salads, then scatter with the chopped fennel fronds and serve.

100g Swiss Brown mushrooms, stalks removed,
caps cut into 3mm-thick slices

100g Portobello mushrooms, stalks removed,
caps cut into 3mm-thick slices

1 King Brown mushroom, very thinly sliced

1 small cauliflower, cut into small florets*

1 clove garlic, any green shoot removed, finely chopped

2 teaspoons thyme leaves

extra virgin olive oil, for cooking

sea salt and freshly ground white pepper

5–6 slices ciabatta bread, crusts removed

3 handfuls baby spinach, washed and spin-dried,
stalks removed

Hazelnut oil vinaigrette

2 eggs, at fridge temperature

1 teaspoon prepared English mustard

sea salt and freshly ground white pepper

60ml hazelnut oil

60ml light olive oil or grapeseed oil

20ml aged white-wine vinegar [preferably Forum
Chardonnay vinegar*], or to taste

Serves 6

An Autumn Salad with Mushrooms & Cauliflower

Sometimes just a few ingredients can deliver a splendid and satisfying dish. The earthy neutrality of the mushrooms blends so well with the cauliflower and is offset by the gentle acidity of spinach. The hazelnut oil vinaigrette brings this gentle salad to life. Serve prior to crumbed veal cutlets with risotto Milanese and green beans. Follow with sliced pears on ice and two cheeses. Real comfort food.

1 Cover the mushrooms with plastic film and refrigerate while the other ingredients are prepared.

2 Soak the cauliflower in very cold water for 10 minutes, then drain and cook in a saucepan of boiling salted water for 1 minute; it should be undercooked but flavoursome. Drain and refresh under cold running water, then drain well. Turn onto a clean dry tea towel to absorb any remaining water.

3 Combine the garlic, thyme leaves and 150ml olive oil and season with salt and pepper. Leave at room temperature for 15–20 minutes, then strain through a fine sieve, reserving the olive oil.

4 Roughly tear the bread into 2cm-long strips. Heat the reserved oil in a deep frying pan until quite hot and fry the bread until pale golden, then tip into a sieve to drain. Drain on paper towel.

5 To make the vinaigrette, prick the eggs with a fine pin and lower into boiling water. Cook for 3 minutes, then drain and refresh under cold running water. Crack the eggs in the centre of the shell over a small mixing bowl and scoop the yolk out into the bowl with a teaspoon. Add the mustard, ¼ teaspoon salt and some pepper and whisk together, then slowly work in the oils as if making a light mayonnaise, adding just enough vinegar to achieve a slightly sharp taste; adjust the seasoning if needed. It should be the texture of thickened whipping cream.

6 Combine the cauliflower, mushrooms and spinach in a large mixing bowl, then moisten with enough vinaigrette to coat the ingredients without them being too wet. Distribute between 6 entrée plates and scatter with the fried bread. Serve immediately.

4 × 1cm-thick slices ciabatta bread, crusts removed

1 tablespoon fresh thyme leaves

1 clove garlic, any green shoot removed, finely chopped

100ml extra virgin olive oil

sea salt and freshly ground black pepper

½ head radicchio, washed and spin-dried, finely shaved

1 handful small rocket sprigs, washed and spin-dried

2 tablespoons flat-leaf parsley leaves, washed and spin-dried, torn

8 large basil leaves, torn

½ cup [50g] walnut kernels, broken

a few drops walnut oil

1 head fennel, outer ribs removed, bulb finely shaved

1 firm Packham or Corella pear, washed, cored and thinly sliced

juice of ½ lemon

4 small Italian buffalo mozzarella cheeses, torn or cut into 1cm-thick pieces

1 small handful chives, cut into 2cm lengths

Vinaigrette

60ml extra virgin olive oil

2 teaspoons aged balsamic vinegar

sea salt and freshly ground black pepper

Serves 4

A Bistro Moncur Mozzarella Salad

Bistro Moncur's menu always features at least one composed salad, and this often incorporates cheese. The beautiful Italian-made buffalo mozzarella opens up endless possibilities as it is mildly flavoured and has a lovely light texture. This salad relies on bitter and sweet flavours combined with the firm texture of raw pears and fennel for its balance. Purchase some high-quality aged balsamic vinegar as this will make all the difference – despite the cost you will find that very little is needed given its strength, and subsequently a bottle will last for a long time.

1 Roughly tear the bread into 2cm pieces. Toss with the thyme leaves, garlic and 50ml of the olive oil, then season lightly with salt and pepper. Heat the remaining olive oil in a frying pan over medium heat until hot but not smoking, then sauté the bread, reducing the heat a little and tossing until golden brown. Discard the garlic and turn the bread onto paper towel to absorb any excess oil. Set aside.

2 Combine the radicchio, rocket, parsley and basil in a large mixing bowl.

3 Toss the walnut pieces with a few drops of walnut oil, then toss in a dry frying pan over medium heat until toasted. Leave to cool.

4 For the vinaigrette, whisk the oil and vinegar with a touch of salt and pepper.

5 Toss the fennel and pear with the lemon juice, then drain.

6 Add the fennel, pear and walnuts to the bowl of leaves, then moisten with most of the vinaigrette and toss with your hands.

7 Distribute the salad between 4 entrée plates, then tuck the mozzarella pieces in here and there, finishing with a few drops of vinaigrette on the mozzarella. Scatter with the bread and chives and serve at once.

4 eggs, at fridge temperature

60ml extra virgin olive oil, plus extra if needed

1 clove garlic, roughly chopped

200g skinless smoked belly bacon or smoked speck, cut into 5mm-thick slices, then into 5mm batons

3 × 1cm-thick slices light sourdough bread, crusts removed

olive oil spray or vegetable oil spray

¼ cup pine nuts

3 bunches spinach, stalks removed, washed several times in cold water and spin-dried, then large leaves torn into bite-sized pieces

Vinaigrette

1 clove garlic, smashed

sea salt and freshly ground white pepper

1 teaspoon Dijon mustard

80ml extra virgin olive oil, or to taste

20ml aged red-wine vinegar [such as Forum Cabernet vinegar*], or to taste

Serves 6

Spinach Salad

The Kings Cross institution Bayswater Brasserie opened in 1982 and I became a regular customer. The chef, my friend Tony Papas, served a wonderful spinach salad that I must have ordered more than fifty times over so many delicious meals there – thanks Tony. Here is my take on this great healthy salad.

1 Prick the eggs with a pin at the wide end, then lower into a saucepan of boiling water for 10 minutes. Drain and refresh under cold running water, then shell them. Separate the yolks from the whites, then roughly chop the whites into 5mm pieces and crumble the yolks.

2 To make the vinaigrette, select a suitably sized salad bowl to allow for tossing the salad with ease at the table. Rub the inside of the bowl with the garlic and discard its debris. Season with ¼ teaspoon salt and a generous amount of pepper, then mix in the mustard. Slowly whisk in the oil until the vinaigrette thickens a little, then add the vinegar, keeping the flavour on the rich side. Taste to check the seasoning.

3 Combine the olive oil with the garlic and leave at room temperature for 15–20 minutes, then strain through a fine sieve, discarding the garlic.

4 Preheat the oven to 100°C. Fry the bacon in a frying pan over medium heat until golden but not hard. Drain and dry with paper towel, then transfer to the warm oven.

5 Tear the bread into 2cm × 1cm strips, toss in the garlic oil, then drain into a small frying pan. Add the remaining oil to the pan, adding extra if needed, then fry the croûtons over medium heat until golden, reducing the temperature so they don't catch. Drain and dry with paper towel.

6 Spray a clean frying pan with ever so little oil and fry the pine nuts over medium and then low heat until golden; keep tossing them since pine nuts burn very easily. Turn onto paper towel to drain.

7 Add the spinach to the vinaigrette and toss gently to coat the leaves. Distribute the croûtons, bacon, egg and pine nuts over the salad. Toss again at the table and serve at once.

1 small cauliflower, cut into small florets*

30ml extra virgin olive oil

250g Slippery Jack mushrooms, stalks and any pine needles discarded, wiped of any dirt with a moistened cloth or paper towel, cut into 5mm-thick slices

sea salt and freshly ground white pepper

1 clove garlic, finely chopped

2 tablespoons finely chopped curly-leaf parsley

250g baby green beans, tops snapped off [leave the tails on]

250g fresh pea pods, shelled

60g walnut kernels, each broken into 4–5 pieces

2 teaspoons walnut oil

1 handful small watercress sprigs, washed and spin-dried

Walnut oil vinaigrette

50ml walnut oil

50ml grapeseed oil

20ml cider vinegar*

a touch lemon juice

sea salt and freshly ground white pepper

Serves 6

Salad of Cauliflower, Mushrooms, Baby Beans & Peas with Walnut Oil Vinaigrette

This entrée salad is at its best in autumn when fresh wild mushrooms are available such as the delicious Slippery Jacks, the Australian equivalent to the French *cèpe* or Italian porcini. Slippery Jack mushrooms should never be washed. Serve this before grilled duck breasts with lentils, roast garlic and eschalots.

1 Place the cauliflower in a bowl of very cold water for 10 minutes to dispel the strong odour of the vegetable. Blanch the drained florets for 1 minute or so in boiling salted water, then drain and refresh under cold running water. Drain well and leave in the colander for 10 minutes, then turn onto a clean dry tea towel to absorb any remaining water.

2 Heat the olive oil in a frying pan over high heat to near smoking point. Add the mushrooms and some salt and pepper and sauté quickly, then reduce the heat to medium and cook until they soften. Toss the pan frequently to disperse the heat evenly. Add the garlic and cook a moment longer, then toss the mushrooms with the parsley and tip onto a plate to cool.

3 Plunge the beans into plenty of well-salted boiling water and cook for 3–5 minutes; they should have a little bite but not be crunchy. Drain and refresh under cold running water, then drain very well.

4 Cook the peas in a saucepan of plenty of well-salted boiling water for 3–5 minutes. Drain and refresh under cold running water, then drain very well.

5 Toss the walnut pieces in the walnut oil, then fry over low heat to gain a touch of colour – take care since they will burn easily. Turn onto paper towel to drain.

6 To make the vinaigrette, whisk the walnut and grapeseed oils with the vinegar and lemon juice. Season lightly, then adjust with lemon juice if necessary; it should taste slightly acidic.

7 Combine the cauliflower, mushrooms, beans, peas and walnuts with the vinaigrette and toss gently. Distribute between 6 deep plates and scatter with the watercress.

2 red peppers

18 thick or 24 thin spears asparagus, trimmed

2 ripe avocados*

best quality extra virgin olive oil, for drizzling

aged balsamic vinegar, for drizzling

sea salt and freshly ground white pepper

Serves 6

Grilled Red Peppers, Asparagus & Avocado – A Simple Salad

For those who believe that less is more, here is a pretty salad calling for the best raw materials available at the market. Use equal proportions of each vegetable and allow enough to cater adequately for those about to enjoy this lovely dish.

1 Grill the peppers over an open gas flame [or better still on a barbecue]. Peel and cut them into 1cm strips, discarding the inner membrane and seeds [never let grilled peppers near water as this diminishes their flavour].

2 Blanch the asparagus in a shallow pan of boiling water for 2–4 minutes, depending on the thickness – it should emerge with some firmness. Refresh under cold running water and drain well, then turn onto a clean tea towel to absorb any remaining water.

3 Cut the avocados in half lengthwise, then remove the stones. Cut the avocados into quarters and peel them, then lay on a chopping board. Cut the avocado sections on the diagonal into 4–5 slices, then arrange on 6 entrée plates.

4 Place a bundle of asparagus around the avocado and finish with the peppers. Splash with the very best olive oil and a few drops of well-aged balsamic vinegar. Scatter with a little flaked salt and a few grinds of coarse white pepper. Serve at once.

6 large Slippery Jack or 3–4 King Brown mushrooms	
6 globe artichokes	
1 lemon, cut into quarters	
80ml extra virgin olive oil	
sea salt flakes and freshly ground white pepper	
20–40ml verjuice* or mild white-wine vinegar	
1 head fennel, top and bottom trimmed, coarse outer ribs removed	
3 tablespoons finely shredded flat-leaf parsley	
shaved parmesan, to serve	

Serves 6

Raw Mushroom, Globe Artichoke Heart & Fennel Salad

This is a dish to prepare in late autumn when artichokes are in season and there is a likelihood that some wild Slippery Jack mushrooms might be available. If you can't find Slippery Jacks then the best cultivated mushroom to use for this dish is the King Brown mushroom, which has a lovely aroma. Prepare the salad just before serving to avoid discolouration of the ingredients.

1   If using Slippery Jacks, discard the stalks and use a moistened cloth to remove any dirt or pine needles. King Brown mushrooms need only have their bases lightly trimmed. Thinly slice the mushrooms and distribute between 6 entrée plates.

2   Pull off most of the leaves from the artichokes, then trim close to their bases [which are known as the hearts]. Immediately rub with cut lemon to prevent discolouration. Cut off the remaining leaves about 15mm from the base and rub the surfaces with lemon. Use a small knife to trim around the edge of each heart. The choke sits on top of the heart and must be removed using a teaspoon in a gentle rotary scooping action; rub with lemon again. Thinly slice the hearts, putting them into a bowl, then add a little lemon juice and 2 teaspoons of the olive oil. Toss the artichoke and distribute over the mushrooms, tossing slightly. Sprinkle with salt, a few grinds of pepper and a drizzle of oil and verjuice.

3   Finely shave the fennel over the salads, then scatter with the parsley and parmesan. Serve immediately.

40ml olive oil	3 × 2cm-thick slices sourdough bread, crusts removed, torn into thin strips
sea salt	60ml extra virgin olive oil, plus extra for drizzling
9 large globe artichokes	4–6 very fresh large cultivated mushrooms, stalks removed, caps very thinly sliced
1 lemon, cut into quarters	1 handful garlic chives or regular chives, finely chopped
freshly ground white pepper	**Serves 6**
juice of 2 large lemons	
1 small clove garlic, smashed	

Raw Globe Artichoke Heart, Mushroom & Garlic Chive Salad with Artichoke Vinaigrette

This is a bit time-consuming but worth the effort since it utilises the interior of the stalks and the flesh of the cooked globe artichoke leaves in a creamy sauce that is spread under the artichoke hearts and mushrooms. Dress simply with your favourite extra virgin olive oil.

1   Preheat the oven to 150°C. Bring a large saucepan of water to the boil with 20ml of the olive oil and salt to taste.

2   Detach and discard the first 2 layers of leaves from the artichokes as well as the stalks, then rub the cut surfaces with lemon to prevent discolouration. Cut off the remaining leaves about 2cm above the bases and reserve. Trim the leaf ends away from the bases [hearts] and scoop out the chokes [hairy, fibrous matter in the centre], then drop each one into some lemon juice to stop them from discolouring. Cook the reserved leaves for about 10 minutes in the pan of water.

3   Meanwhile, cut the stalks into 2 or 3 pieces, then boil for 10–15 minutes. Drain, then refresh under cold running water. Split the stalks lengthwise, then scoop their interiors into a bowl.

4   Use a small spoon to scoop the flesh off the leaves into a mortar and add the interior of the stalks. Using a pestle, mash the flesh to a paste with the remaining olive oil and season with salt, pepper and lemon juice. If the texture is too thick, then dilute with a little cold water to achieve a pouring cream consistency.

5   Rub inside a mixing bowl with the garlic then discard the debris. Put the bread into the bowl, then moisten with the extra virgin olive oil, tossing well. Turn the bread into an ovenproof frying pan or roasting pan and toast in the oven, tossing frequently, until golden. Set aside to cool.

6   Spread a very thin layer of the artichoke sauce over 6 flat entrée plates using a tablespoon.

7   Cut the artichoke hearts into 3mm-thick slices, toss them in lemon juice, then pat dry. Scatter one-sixth of the artichoke and mushroom over the vinaigrette. Drizzle a little extra virgin olive oil over each salad and scatter with the croûtons and the chives, then serve.

24–30 spears white asparagus		**Vinaigrette**
sea salt		150ml extra virgin olive oil
3 eggs, at fridge temperature		30ml almond oil or walnut oil
40g flaked almonds		20–40ml lemon juice
vegetable or olive oil spray		sea salt and freshly ground white pepper
⅓ cup finely chopped curly-leaf parsley		the very tiniest pinch cayenne pepper
		Serves 6

White Asparagus Salad with Egg Mimosa & Toasted Flaked Almonds

White asparagus is the same plant as green asparagus, the difference being that it is mounded with soil as it grows and the resultant absence of sunlight prevents it from becoming green. Faux white asparagus is grown under a covering of black plastic and is less bitter than that grown under mounds of earth. True white asparagus offers a distinct bitterness that is not to everyone's palate. White asparagus is generally dressed with mayonnaise or vinaigrette. When served hot it is commonly dressed with butter then cooked until brown to develop a rich, nutty flavour that counteracts the bitterness. Hollandaise sauce is also a very good accompaniment for hot white asparagus.

Here the addition of hard-boiled egg yolk and white pressed separately through a sieve [this is known as mimosa, see page 74], finely chopped parsley and toasted almonds has a lovely harmony with the bitterness of the white asparagus.

1   Preheat the oven to 150°C. Peel the thicker part of each asparagus spear with a vegetable peeler, then drop into a bowl of cold water.

2   Bring a large, wide frying pan of water to the boil, add salt to taste and simmer the asparagus over medium heat for 6–8 minutes or until tender when pierced with a knife tip; it should remain a little firm. This step may need to be carried out in 2 batches since it is best to cook the asparagus in a single layer to prevent it from overcooking.

3   Transfer the asparagus to a bowl and briefly refresh under cold running water to avoid them absorbing too much water. Drain in a colander for at least 10 minutes. Place on paper towel to absorb the remaining water.

4   Prick the eggs with a pin at the wide end, then gently lower into a saucepan of boiling water and cook for 10 minutes. Drain and refresh under cold running water. Leave to cool, then scoop out the yolks and press through a sieve into a bowl. Press the whites through a sieve into another bowl and set aside.

5   Spray the almonds lightly with oil, then toss and toast on a baking tray in the oven until pale golden; toss several times to ensure they colour evenly.

6   To make the vinaigrette, whisk all of the ingredients together.

7   Divide the asparagus between 6 flat plates and moisten with the vinaigrette, then scatter with the sieved whites and yolks, finishing with the parsley and almonds.

2 eggplants [aubergines], cut crosswise into 12 × 1cm-thick slices	1 good handful mizuna or baby rocket leaves, washed and spin-dried
sea salt	black olive tapenade, to serve
100ml extra virgin olive oil	**Vinaigrette**
3 zucchini [courgettes], cut lengthwise into 1cm-thick slices	2 teaspoons coriander seeds
2 red peppers	1 small clove garlic, any green shoot removed, finely chopped
36 basil leaves [from about 1 large bunch]	1 small fresh birds eye chilli, seeded and finely chopped
100ml olive oil or vegetable oil	100ml extra virgin olive oil
1 litre water	20ml Banyuls* or best quality aged red-wine vinegar [such as Forum Cabernet vinegar*], or to taste
1 teaspoon white-wine vinegar	sea salt and freshly ground black pepper
6 eggs, at fridge temperature	**Serves 6**
1 red onion, sliced into very thin rings	
3–4 Ox Heart or Roma tomatoes,* cut into 1.5cm chunks	

Salad of Grilled Vegetables Provençale

I love making ratatouille and thought that its ingredients could make a delicious salad, albeit a seriously untraditional one. The blend of eggplant, zucchini, peppers and olives laced with tomatoes is so summery and appetising; add a soft poached egg and a touch of tapenade for a lovely entrée salad. Some of the ingredients are raw, providing a contrast to the grilled vegetables. Use a mandoline* for ease in slicing the vegetables.

I generally dislike dishes that consist of stacked ingredients since they are awkward to eat. However, this recipe lends itself to stacking so that the flavours mingle on the palate as a whole. This dish sits well alongside barbecued lamb or pork cutlets or simply serve it for lunch as a dish in its own right, followed by a bowl of crisp leaves and finishing with cheese and fruit.

1 Dust the eggplant slices with salt on both sides and place in a colander for 1 hour to drain off the juices. Wipe off the salt and dry the slices with paper towel. Heat a cast-iron chargrill to very hot, then brush the slices with a little olive oil. Grill on both sides until soft but not falling apart, reducing the temperature as needed to avoid burning. As they are cooked, transfer the slices to a paper towel-lined tray.

2 Brush the zucchini with a little of the olive oil, then grill on both sides until soft but not falling apart, reducing the temperature as needed to avoid burning. As they are cooked, transfer to a paper towel-lined tray.

3 Grill the peppers under a very hot overhead griller, then peel off the skins, trim off the tops and bottoms, and remove the seeds and membrane. Cut into 1cm-thick strips.

4 Tear half the basil leaves into small pieces and set aside. Heat the olive or vegetable oil in a saucepan over medium heat until quite hot but not at all near smoking point and, working in batches, deep-fry the remaining basil leaves; this will only take seconds so watch closely. Drain on paper towel.

5 Bring the water to the boil in a saucepan with the vinegar. Meanwhile, crack an egg into a cup and have a bowl of iced water at the ready. When the water boils, swirl it with a table knife to create a whirlpool into which you quickly slip an egg. Wait for 20 seconds for the egg to begin to set before adding another egg. Allow to simmer for 2½ minutes. Use a slotted spoon to retrieve the eggs and transfer to a bowl of iced water. Drain on a clean tea towel or paper towel. Remove any debris from the water, then repeat with the remaining eggs.

6 To make the vinaigrette, toast the coriander seeds in a dry frying pan over medium heat until they are aromatic, then turn onto a plate to cool. Grind to a powder with a mortar and pestle or spice mill. Sift the ground coriander to remove any husks. Mix together the garlic, chilli, oil, vinegar, salt and pepper to taste – aim for slightly acidic. Add enough ground coriander to flavour the vinaigrette.

7 To assemble each plate, distribute the eggplant, zucchini, unfried basil and tomato in stacks that will support the poached eggs. Moisten each layer with a little vinaigrette. Place the eggs on top, then scatter over onion and finish with a little tapenade. Scatter the salads with the fried basil, then serve.

6–8 green peppers

sea salt flakes and freshly ground black pepper

80–125ml extra virgin olive oil

2 teaspoons white-wine vinegar

2 × 47.5g cans Ortiz* anchovy fillets, drained, each fillet cut in half lengthwise

Serves 4

Peppers à la Toulonnaise

I came across this lovely little salad in the 1953 publication *True Provençal and Niçoise Cooking* by Jean-Noël Escudier and Peta Fuller. The charm of this salad lies in the simplicity of its ingredients. Serve as an entrée or as an hors d'oeuvre, perhaps with celeriac rémoulade, sliced prosciutto or spicy salami and a bowl of olives [as pictured here]. I have taken the liberty of adapting the original method, adding salt and pepper and not washing the cooked peppers as suggested by the authors.

1 Preheat the oven to 250°C. Cover an oven shelf with foil, folding it on either side under the rails. Roast the peppers directly on the foil, turning them as they are blistered with brown and black patches. Place in a plastic freezer bag for 15 minutes or so to sweat and loosen the skins. Carefully peel the peppers by hand. Use a moistened paper towel to remove any tiny burnt particles that remain.

2 Cut the peppers in half lengthwise, then remove the seeds and membrane. Cut into long 5mm-thick strips and arrange on a small platter. Season very lightly with salt and some pepper.

3 Mix the oil and vinegar and drizzle over the peppers, then decorate with the anchovies in a crisscross pattern. Refrigerate for several hours, then leave at room temperature for 20 minutes before serving.

ice cubes	**Pistou**
6 large vine-ripened tomatoes, ripe but on the firm side	2 cloves garlic, peeled
extra virgin olive oil	sea salt
salt	pinch dried chilli flakes
1 teaspoon white-wine vinegar	2 large handfuls basil leaves
6 egg yolks	80ml extra virgin olive oil
6 basil leaves	freshly ground black pepper
2 heads baby fennel, outer ribs removed [retain some of the fronds if still attached], cut in half lengthwise	**Serves 6**
a little lemon juice	
1 teaspoon olive oil	
2 teaspoons verjuice*	

Roasted Tomato with Pistou, Poached Egg Yolk & Fennel

This attractive dish makes a lovely first entrée salad as part of a formal four-course meal. The flavours are pure and the dish offers enough acidity to stimulate the appetite for the courses to follow. *Pistou* is the French cousin to Italian pesto and traditionally consists of garlic, basil, olive oil and seasonings.

1   Preheat the oven to 150°C. Bring a large saucepan of water to the boil and have a large bowl of iced water ready.

2   Cut a little shallow cross in the top of each tomato, then blanch 2 at a time in the boiling water for 10 seconds. Transfer to the iced water with a slotted spoon, then gently squeeze off the skins. Pat dry with paper towel.

3   Brush the tomatoes with olive oil and season with salt, using a salt shaker to coat evenly. Place a small cake-cooling rack in a baking dish and put the tomatoes on the rack. Roast for 20 minutes or until slightly scorched. Leave them to cool on the rack; do not refrigerate them. Use a metal spatula or cake slice to transfer the tomatoes to 6 small entrée plates.

4   To make the pistou, put the garlic in a small saucepan of cold water and bring to the boil. Drain and repeat, then refresh under cold running water. Crush the garlic on a chopping board (remove any green shoot) with a little salt and the chilli flakes, using the flat side of a knife blade to make a paste, then transfer to a mortar. Add the basil leaves and, using a pestle, work to a paste, adding a few drops of oil at a time. Check the seasoning. Work in the remaining oil and finish with pepper.

5   Using a sharp knife, cut a slice from the top of each tomato. Scoop out and discard about 1 teaspoonful of cooked tomato flesh to create a cavity large enough to accommodate a poached egg yolk. Sprinkle a little salt and pistou into each cavity.

6   Bring some water and vinegar to the boil in a sauté pan and poach 1 egg yolk at a time for 1 minute, then slip it into the bowl of iced water. The yolk should be just set enough to keep it together. Use a slotted spoon to retrieve each yolk and carefully pat it dry with a tissue. Place a basil leaf across the cavity in each tomato, then place the yolk on top.

7   Shave the fennel thinly using a mandoline.* Transfer to a bowl with a very little lemon juice and toss with the olive oil. Arrange the fennel around each tomato.

8   Dilute the remaining pistou with the verjuice, whisking to combine; it will not emulsify. Drizzle the pistou around each tomato and serve. Store any remaining pistou in the fridge and use within a few days.

3 litres water	best quality extra virgin olive oil
1 tablespoon salt	6 small Roma tomatoes, washed
2kg broad beans in pods, shelled [separate the large and smaller beans]	sea salt flakes and freshly ground black pepper
1 baguette [preferably a traditional French one, not sourdough]	8 sprigs [about 1 bunch] French tarragon, leaves roughly snipped
1 large clove garlic, any green shoot removed, lightly smashed	**Serves 6**

Broad Beans on Toast

Here is a simple salad inspired by Sean Moran's superb dish of broad beans on toast. Allow plenty of time for the pleasurable task of double-shelling the broad beans since this is essential to the success of the dish.

1 Preheat the oven to 150°C. Bring the water to the boil, then add the salt. Cook the larger broad beans for 2 minutes after the water returns to the boil. Turn off the heat and, using a slotted spoon, lift them out of the water to drain in a colander, then refresh under cold running water. Drain again. Return the water to the boil. Cook the smaller beans for about 1 minute, then refresh and drain as above.

2 Pinch off the broad bean husks and discard them.

3 Cut the baguette on the diagonal into 7mm-thick slices and lay on a baking tray. Bake for 5–8 minutes to achieve the palest colour [the bread should not be too dry]. Remove from the oven and rub each piece with the garlic and brush with olive oil.

4 Distribute the toast slices between 6 flat entrée plates. Cut the tomatoes into 5mm-thick slices and distribute between the plates. Season with salt and pepper, then drizzle with olive oil and scatter with half the tarragon. Distribute the broad beans casually over the tomato, anoint generously with more olive oil, and finish with the remaining tarragon.

Sean's Broad Beans on Toast

I have fond memories of a winter Sunday's lunch at Sean's Panaroma at Bondi Beach in New South Wales, where Sean Moran served a generous pile of broad beans on toast anointed with a superb Reserve Nolans Road extra virgin olive oil – that was all and a true lesson in the adage that 'less is more'! Of course, the key to the refinement of Sean's dish was the double-shelling of the broad beans to release the verdant inner beans in all their glory. The tiniest beans may be left unshelled, since the pods have not developed the furry texture typical of larger broad beans.

Incidentally, should you come across tiny broad beans with pods no thicker than about 1cm, they may be cooked and eaten whole and taste delicious simply with salt flakes and a scrap of butter.

Composed Salads

1 Lebanese cucumber, peeled and cut into
3mm-thick slices

ice cubes

300g baby green beans, tops snapped off
[leave the tails on], cut in half

300g baby butter beans, tops snapped off
[leave the tails on]

6 cornichons,* finely diced

1 tablespoon wholegrain mustard

120ml crème fraîche*

20ml lemon juice, or to taste

sea salt and freshly ground white pepper

200g smoked leg ham or gypsy ham, cut into
5mm-thick matchsticks

3–4 radicchio leaves, washed and spin-dried,
very finely shredded

Serves 6

Green & Butter Bean Salad with Smoked Leg Ham & Creamy Wholegrain Mustard Dressing

The slightly sweet flavour of the beans is given body by the smoked ham and tang by the mustard-seed dressing. Freshness from the crisp cucumber and bitterness from the shaved radicchio make this a very satisfying entrée salad.

1 Soak the sliced cucumber in a bowl of iced water for 20 minutes, then drain and dry thoroughly with paper towel.

2 Blanch the green and butter beans separately in plenty of boiling salted water for 3–4 minutes so they are slightly crisp, then drain and refresh under cold running water. Drain well and pat dry with paper towel if necessary.

3 Mix the cornichons, mustard, crème fraîche and lemon juice in a small bowl, then season to taste. If the dressing thickens, dilute with a little cold water.

4 Pour most of the dressing into a wide bowl, then add the cucumber, beans, ham and radicchio. Toss gently using your hands, adding more dressing as required. Serve at once.

12 spears asparagus

1–2 heads baby fennel, outer ribs removed, base and stalks trimmed

extra virgin olive oil

2 teaspoons balsamic vinegar

lemon juice, to taste

sea salt

200ml peanut oil or grapeseed oil

2 cups flat-leaf parsley leaves, washed and very well dried

12 × 55g eggs, at fridge temperature

½ quantity Aïoli [see page 71]

freshly ground grains of paradise or white pepper

Serves 6 or as part of antipasto

Del Posto's Asparagus & Fried Egg Salad

Del Posto is one of New York's outstanding modern Italian restaurants, and I tasted this salad as part of their antipasto selection. The fried egg was dusted with an exotically flavoured pepper and surrounded by a salad of finely shaved raw asparagus and deep-fried flat-leaf parsley with drops of aïoli – a brilliant creation. In thinking about how I might develop this idea as an entrée salad, I have added shaved fennel for a fresh aromatic touch and crunchy croûtons for more texture. Herbie's Spices※ have a wide range of peppers so I tasted a few recently and selected grains of paradise [also known as melegueta pepper or long pepper] from the west coast of Africa. It has the same cardamom character and numbingly hot, slightly bitter flavour I recall tasting at Del Posto.

1 Shave the asparagus into 3mm-thick slices with a sharp knife, setting aside the tops to garnish, then shave the fennel to about the same thickness. Moisten with enough olive oil to coat, the balsamic vinegar and a few drops of lemon juice and toss well. Distribute between 6 flat entrée plates, then sprinkle lightly with salt.

2 Heat 160ml of the oil in a small deep saucepan until quite hot but not smoking. Fry the parsley in 3 or 4 batches for 10 seconds or until crisp. Drain on paper towel.

3 Heat a wide-based frying pan with a smear of oil, then fry 2 or 3 eggs at a time until the whites are crisp, then drain on paper towel.

4 Place 2 good teaspoonfuls of aïoli in small clearings made within the salads, then place 2 eggs on each salad, finishing by dusting the eggs lightly with ground grains of paradise. Scatter the fried parsley over the salads, garnish with asparagus tops and serve immediately.

2 firm eating apples, peeled, cored and cut into quarters [to yield 200g]

juice of 1 lemon

150g pecan nuts, chopped into 4–5 pieces each

300g smoked turkey, cut into 5mm-thick matchsticks

150g celeriac, cut into 5cm-long matchsticks

2–3 pale inner stalks celery, cut into 5mm dice [to yield 100g]

½ teaspoon sweet paprika

1 handful small watercress sprigs, washed and spin-dried

1 handful baby rocket sprigs, washed and spin-dried

Mayonnaise

1 yolk from a hard-boiled egg [see page 8], worked to a paste with a fork

2 egg yolks

½ teaspoon English mustard

sea salt and freshly ground white pepper

tiniest pinch cayenne pepper

75ml grapeseed oil

75ml walnut oil

10–20ml verjuice*

lemon juice, to taste

Serves 6

Smoked Turkey Salad

Good-quality smoked turkey is readily available and a lovely salad can be assembled around it without too much fuss, using ingredients drawn from the Waldorf salad tradition. Slicing and cutting the vegetables will be so quick if you use a mandoline.* Smoked chicken may be substituted for the turkey with excellent results. Watercress and baby rocket sprigs provide the perfect greens to complete this salad. Suitable for a buffet or as an entrée prior to grilled fish served with a mixed leaf salad.

1 Thinly slice the apple and toss with lemon juice. Strain the lemon juice and set aside for making the mayonnaise. Combine the apple, pecan nuts, smoked turkey, celeriac and celery in a large bowl.

2 To make the mayonnaise, combine the egg yolk paste with the raw yolks, mustard, salt, pepper and cayenne and then whisk well. Slowly add the combined oils in a fine stream, whisking continuously and taking care not to add more oil before the previous addition is absorbed. Continue adding the remaining oil until quite thick, then add the verjuice and enough of the reserved lemon juice to acidulate and season to taste. The texture should be thick enough to coat the salad ingredients.

3 Bind the apple, nuts, turkey, celeriac and celery with just enough mayonnaise to hold them together. Taste and adjust the seasoning; there should be just a hint of cayenne, which will be felt at the back of the palate.

4 Transfer to a wide salad bowl or small platter, dust lightly with paprika, then garnish with watercress and rocket sprigs. Serve immediately.

750g pickled lambs' tongues, soaked in 4 changes of cold water for 1 hour in total

Court-bouillon

1.7 litres cold water

300ml dry white wine

20ml tarragon vinegar

1 onion, sliced

1 carrot, sliced

2 stalks celery, white part only, sliced

bouquet garni* [10 parsley stalks, 6 sprigs thyme, 1 bay leaf, 3 strips lemon zest and 10 cracked black peppercorns all wrapped in a muslin cloth and tied with kitchen twine]

3 teaspoons sea salt

Salad

1 pink grapefruit

¼ cup mustard fruit* figs, thinly sliced

4–6 cornichons,* thinly sliced lengthwise

3–4 handfuls mixed salad leaves [including watercress, ribbons of radicchio, witlof tips and mizuna], washed and spin-dried [except the witlof]

½ cup flat-leaf parsley leaves, washed and spin-dried, torn

1 handful chives [about 1 bunch], finely chopped

¼ cup French tarragon leaves, lightly snipped

1 handful chervil sprigs [about ½ bunch], washed and dried

½ cup [75g] hazelnuts

Vinaigrette

1 egg, at fridge temperature

1 clove garlic, smashed

2 teaspoons wholegrain mustard

sea salt and freshly ground pepper

40ml hazelnut oil

40ml grapeseed oil

1 teaspoon finely grated lemon zest

2 teaspoons lemon juice or aged sherry vinegar

Serves 6

Salad of Pickled Lambs' Tongues

Pickled lambs' tongues have a delicate sweetness and lovely pink hue. A cooperative butcher will pickle the lambs' tongues for you, but you will need to order them well in advance. Meat inspectors are obliged to check the health of this offal and tend to slash each tongue carelessly, which can make it difficult to carve attractive slices. Serve prior to fish or poultry.

1   Bring all the court-bouillon ingredients slowly to the boil in a stockpot; skim and then simmer for 20 minutes. Strain through a fine sieve and correct the seasoning, keeping the saltiness of the tongues in mind. Simmer the tongues in the court-bouillon for 1¼–1½ hours or until tender when pierced with a fine skewer. Drain in a colander over a bowl, keeping the court-bouillon, then peel the tongues while still warm. Trim away the root ends and any stubborn pieces of skin then cover with court-bouillon. Cool at room temperature before refrigerating.

2   To make the salad, trim the skin from the top and bottom of the grapefruit and place a cut surface on a chopping board. Using a sharp paring knife, slice off the skin following the natural contour of the fruit so as produce an evenly rounded finish. Hold the grapefruit in one hand and slice between the pith and segments over a bowl to collect the juices. Cut each segment into 2 or 3 thin slices, then put them into the collected juice.

3   Add the mustard fruits to the cornichons. Place the leaves and herbs in a large mixing bowl, then cover and refrigerate.

4   Preheat the oven 160°C. Toast the hazelnuts on a baking tray for 10 minutes or until the skins begin to split. Turn into a coarse sieve and, with the aid of a clean tea towel, rub off the skins; it is often difficult to remove all the skin so just do the best you can. Roughly chop and return to the oven to give them some colour, then set aside.

5   For the vinaigrette, prick the egg with a fine pin and cook in boiling water for 3 minutes. Meanwhile, rub the surface of a small mixing bowl with the garlic, then discard the debris. Crack the egg over the bowl and scoop out the yolk, then whisk in the mustard, ¼ teaspoon salt and some pepper. Gradually work in the oils to make a slightly thickened vinaigrette. Add the lemon zest. Adjust the seasoning with salt, pepper, lemon juice or vinegar, keeping it on the sharp side.

6   Drain the tongues, discarding the court-bouillon, then thinly slice them lengthwise.

7   Moisten the leaves and herbs with half the vinaigrette and toss gently with your hands, then distribute between 6 deep entrée plates. Drain the sliced grapefruit and combine with the tongue, then moisten with vinaigrette, tossing gently. Arrange among the leaves, finishing with the mustard fruit, cornichons and hazelnuts. Drizzle with the last of the vinaigrette and serve immediately.

3 × 300g herring fillets in oil [preferably Eskal-brand Matjes]

2 small carrots, thinly sliced

2 small red onions, thinly sliced into rings

1 tablespoon thyme leaves

3 small bay leaves

2 teaspoons green peppercorns [rinsed if tinned]

2 teaspoons fennel seeds

6 strips scrubbed lemon rind

150ml light olive oil, or to cover the herrings

Potato salad

800g kipfler potatoes, washed

sea salt and freshly ground white pepper

a good splash dry white wine

60ml extra virgin olive oil

½ cup chopped curly-leaf parsley

1 large handful chives, snipped

3–4 hard-boiled eggs [see page 8], shelled and very roughly chopped

Serves 6–8

Herrings with Potato Salad

Marinated herrings served with the simplest potato salad, or even just waxy potatoes dressed with olive oil and some parsley, are at the very heart of French bistro cuisine. While recently in Paris, I dined at Chez Georges in the 2nd arrondisement. This is one of the few original bistros where little has changed in terms of the style of service – which, incidentally, is provided by highly efficient women of a certain age under the direction of the male patron. I was excited to find *Salade de pommes de terre aux harengs* while perusing the authentic bistro fare. A plate of very simple potato salad arrived, followed by a gleaming white terrine filled with herring fillets and service cutlery, the idea being that guests just help themselves to as much as they like. This is in keeping with the real tradition of bistro hospitality that one finds less and less in France and certainly not at home.

It is worth noting that the herrings will need to be marinated for three days before you wish to serve this salad.

1 Drain the herrings and rinse under cold running water, then drain well and pat dry.

2 Place the fillets in layers in a non-reactive airtight container, distributing the other ingredients as equally as possible and pouring enough oil between the layers and on top to cover them by 1cm. Seal well and refrigerate for 3 days to mature.

3 For the potato salad, bring the potatoes to the boil in plenty of boiling salted water and simmer for 20 minutes or until they are fairly easy to pierce using a fine skewer. They must not be too soft or the salad will end up more like a rough mess. Drain and peel the potatoes with your fingertips as soon as they can be handled. As each potato is peeled, transfer it to a covered bowl to keep warm. Slice the potatoes into 1cm-thick rings and place on a wide platter, then season and drizzle sparingly with the wine. Shake gently so as not to break them, then moisten fairly generously with olive oil. Scatter with the herbs and egg, then use your hands to gently combine everything.

4 Drain the herring and discard the marinade. Pat the fillets dry and pack into an attractive serving dish. Transfer the potato salad to a serving dish and serve.

24–30 live yabbies, placed in the freezer for about 20 minutes	80ml grapeseed oil
	30ml hazelnut oil
Court-bouillon	20ml lime juice, or to taste
250ml dry white wine	tiniest pinch cayenne pepper
1 small onion, sliced	freshly ground white pepper
½ stalk celery, washed and sliced	**Salad**
½ small carrot, sliced	2 heads baby fennel, outer ribs discarded, halved lengthwise
bouquet garni* [a few sprigs fresh thyme, 1 bay leaf and 2 strips lemon zest all wrapped in a muslin cloth and tied with kitchen twine]	juice of ½ lemon
	1–2 pale inner stalks celery, cut into 3mm-thick slices
1.75 litres cold water	1 small head white witlof
1½ tablespoons sea salt, or to taste	1 head red witlof
Hazelnut vinaigrette	2 large avocados,* peeled and cut lengthwise into 6 segments
1 egg, at fridge temperature	1 small handful chives, cut into 2cm lengths
¼ teaspoon sea salt	**Serves 6**
2 teaspoons Dijon mustard	

Salad of Yabbies, Fennel, Celery & Avocado with Hazelnut Vinaigrette

A yabby feast may still be a tradition for Australian farmers with a dam on their properties. An old farmer told me a story about the days when bags of yabbies were taken to a picnic site and cooked in a forty-four gallon drum over an open fire and served with a slab of canned beer for each bloke. This was followed by pavlova. Certainly not the sort of picnic one might imagine for city folk!

Yabbies have a deliciously sweet, slightly muddy flavour that blends well with the freshness of fennel and celery. The hazelnut oil dressing matches the muddy character of these very delicate shellfish. A splendid entrée for any menu that might offer a whole baked fish to follow such as Murray cod stuffed with eschalots and sorrel. And why not serve a passionfruit pavlova to give the meal a truly Australian touch?

1   While the yabbies are in the freezer, bring the court-bouillon ingredients slowly to the boil in a stockpot, skim, then simmer for 20–30 minutes. Strain directly into a 3–4 litre stockpot and check the seasoning for saltiness.

2   Meanwhile, start to prepare the vinaigrette. Prick the egg with a pin, then cook in boiling water for 3 minutes. Drain and refresh under cold running water.

3   Cook the yabbies in 4 batches in the boiling court-bouillon for 1 minute, transferring each batch to a large bowl or tray to cool at room temperature.

4   Snap off the yabby claws, reserving 18 to garnish, then crack gently using a rolling pin. Holding one yabby body in one hand and the tail in the other, carefully twist the tail to release it from the body, then repeat with the remaining yabbies. The digestive tract will generally dislodge from the tail if the tail is detached slowly. Break away each side of the shell with your fingertips, then pull away the shell underneath and dislodge the flesh. Gently pull out and discard any digestive tract. Cover with plastic film and chill if this is done ahead of time [or to maintain flavour, place the tails over a bowl of ice for up to 1 hour].

5   To make the vinaigrette, hold the egg over a small mixing bowl, crack the shell and scoop the yolk into the bowl, then whisk in the salt and mustard. Add the oils slowly in a thin, steady stream [as if making a mayonnaise], then add enough lime juice to make a fresh-tasting vinaigrette, finishing with the cayenne pepper; taste and adjust the seasoning.

6   Thinly shave the fennel using a mandoline* or very sharp knife and toss with the lemon juice, then turn into a sieve to drain. Add the celery to the fennel and moisten with vinaigrette.

7   Cut 3cm tips from 12 smaller witlof leaves, then thinly slice the rest lengthwise. Add them to the other vegetables and toss with the vinaigrette.

8   Place 2 wedges of avocado in the centre of each plate, then equally distribute the salad and yabby tails, finishing with 3 reserved claws per serve. Scatter with the chives, then serve immediately.

Composed Salads

2kg cooked whole mudcrabs or 1.5kg cooked whole blue swimmer crabs or 300–400g cooked crabmeat

3 × 2cm-thick slices day-old sourdough bread, crusts removed, torn into thin strips

225ml extra virgin olive oil

¼ cup tiny salted capers, soaked in warm water then rinsed and dried with paper towel

2–3 tablespoons roughly chopped fennel fronds [optional]

400g short pasta [such as orecchiette, fusilli or strozzapreti]

3–4 cloves garlic, any green shoot removed, coarsely chopped

2–3 fresh red chillies, seeds removed [optional], finely chopped

1 large handful wild rocket leaves, stalks removed, washed and spin-dried

sea salt [optional] and freshly ground black pepper

Serves 6

Warm Pasta & Crab Salad with Chilli & Wild Rocket

This slightly extravagant salad is perfect offered as an entrée in summer before barbecued sirloin steaks and a mixed leaf salad. Thin fusilli or the Benedetto Cavalieri-brand orecchiette or small twirled shapes called strozzapreti [literally meaning 'priest stranglers'] are great for this salad. Use either cooked mudcrabs or blue swimmers and pick the flesh yourself or buy the cooked and ready-picked meat, which is usually sold frozen since it is so perishable. Garlic, chilli and rocket are cooked in extra virgin olive oil to form the foundation flavour for the pasta, which will come to life when tossed with the crabmeat, while the crisp bread brings another texture to play in the salad.

1 Pick the meat from the crabs, taking care to discard any tiny pieces of shell. If using ready-picked crabmeat also check for scraps of shell. Keep chilled in the fridge on a tray rather than in a bowl [the crab will come to room temperature faster if spread out] until 10 minutes before tossing the salad.

2 Preheat the oven to 150°C. Place the bread in a mixing bowl. Moisten generously with 100ml of the olive oil, then toss to coat, transfer to a baking tray and bake for 10 minutes or until nicely coloured; shake the tray from time to time. Leave to cool on the tray, then combine with the capers and fennel fronds, if using. This will be scattered over the salad once the pasta has cooled.

3 Cook the pasta in a saucepan of boiling salted water for a minute or so less than directed on the packet; the pasta should be quite al dente. Reduce the oven temperature to 80°C.

4 While the pasta is cooking, warm a salad bowl in the oven. Heat the remaining olive oil in a saucepan and cook the garlic and chilli over low heat for a moment, then add the rocket, stirring constantly until it wilts. Add the crabmeat and stir to warm it slightly, then add the drained pasta and toss well, adding seasoning to taste; probably little or no salt will be needed.

5 Turn into the warmed salad bowl and cool to room temperature. Scatter with the toasted bread mixture and serve.

1 small head garlic	**Vinaigrette**
30ml extra virgin olive oil	30g Roquefort, rind removed
sea salt	20ml walnut oil
12 × 5mm-thick slices from a baguette or ciabatta, crusts removed	80ml extra virgin olive oil
	20ml crème fraîche* or mild natural yoghurt
2 butter lettuces, washed and spin-dried, torn into smaller pieces	20ml aged red-wine vinegar [such as Banyuls* or Forum Cabernet vinegar*], or to taste
2 handfuls small watercress sprigs, washed and spin-dried	**Serves 6**
1 Josephine or Packham pear, slightly under-ripe	
200g Roquefort, rind removed, crumbled	
freshly ground white pepper	

Roquefort & Butter Lettuce Salad with Roasted Garlic Chapons

Roquefort is considered the king of blue cheeses as it combines a balance between salt and acidity with a superior creamy texture. The lingering mustiness results from its aging in the limestone caves of Cambalou, close to the town of Roquefort-sur-Soulzon in the south-west of France. This is a province where truffles and foie gras abound, as well as the delicious Monbazillac dessert wine.

I recall a brilliant Roquefort and butter lettuce salad served in a smart London hotel where the cheese was baked in a crisp olive oil pastry. This stood majestically surrounded by a salad of soft butter lettuce lightly dressed with a creamy Roquefort vinaigrette. *Chapon* is the name given in Gascony to a slice of bread or croûton rubbed with garlic. Here I've used it to sit under the leaves, providing a great burst of flavour and textural contrast.

While this is a perfect entrée to serve prior to roast chicken [see opposite] it is also excellent to follow roasted game birds such as squab pigeon or pheasant, especially if there is a little of the roasting juices left to add to the vinaigrette; the marriage between the game and leaves is really delicious. Halve the quantities of the vinaigrette if serving the salad as an entrée or to follow a main.

1 Preheat the oven to 150°C. Check the firmness of the garlic; discard any cloves that feel spongy. Rub the garlic head lightly with olive oil and wrap in foil, then bake for 30 minutes or until the garlic is tender when a knife blade is inserted.

2 Remove the foil and separate the cloves, then press them through a sieve directly into a small bowl. Add the remaining olive oil and a touch of salt, then work into a smooth wet paste.

3 Spread the garlic paste on one side of each slice of bread, then bake until slightly coloured but not hard and dry. These are the chapons that will sit underneath the leaves.

4 To make the vinaigrette, using a spoon, crush the Roquefort with the walnut oil. Whisk in the remaining ingredients to achieve a smooth, creamy texture.

5 Place the lettuce and watercress in a large mixing bowl. Dress with half the vinaigrette and toss with your hands. Place 2 slightly warm chapons in the centre of 6 deep plates, then distribute some of the leaves on top.

6 Peel, core and slice the pear very thinly into the bowl of leaves and toss well, then distribute between the salads. Scatter with the crumbled Roquefort, finishing with the remaining vinaigrette and a few grinds of pepper. Serve at once.

1 large eggplant [aubergine], cut lengthwise into 1cm-thick slices

sea salt

80ml extra virgin olive oil, plus extra for cooking

400g fusilli

6 fully ripened tomatoes, roughly cut into 1cm chunks

200g firm full-cream ricotta, crumbled

1 handful basil leaves, gently torn into small pieces

freshly ground black pepper

Serves 6

Salad of Fusilli with Eggplant, Ricotta & Raw Tomato

A room-temperature pasta salad can be a welcome entrée in hot weather, provided it is kept simple. Tossing the hot pasta with raw tomato, fine olive oil and basil is about as easy as it gets, yet this dish is very satisfying. I recall eating such a salad on a hot summer's night at Armando Percuoco's Pulcinella Restaurant in the early 1980s. Armando cooked the linguine rather al dente and tossed it with tomato full of summer sunshine.

My recipe calls for thin fusilli [meaning 'spring-shaped'], which have the advantage of holding the softer ingredients within their crevices. Personally, I would not serve it as a main course simply because it can be a bit heavy to eat as a large portion and, consequently, perhaps a little boring. On the other hand, a small serve seems just right.

1 Put the eggplant in a colander, sprinkle with salt and place a plate on top to compress. Leave to drain for up to 45 minutes, then dry each slice well with paper towel.

2 Preheat the oven to 80°C. Heat a cast-iron chargrill or heavy-based frying pan over medium heat and brush the eggplant slices lightly with olive oil. Cook over medium heat until the eggplant is soft and slightly caramelised. Transfer to a plate and use a fork to break each slice into small pieces. Cover and keep warm in the oven.

3 Cook the fusilli in a saucepan of boiling salted water for a minute or so less than directed on the packet; the pasta should be quite al dente.

4 Drain the fusilli and tip into a large mixing bowl, then add the warm eggplant, tomato, ricotta and basil. Anoint with the olive oil and some pepper, then toss well; be careful – too much oil will only make the salad heavy. Leave to cool to room temperature, then transfer to a deep platter or salad bowl and serve.

3 eggs, at fridge temperature

1 teaspoon celery seeds

3 Lebanese cucumbers, peeled and cut into 3–4 cm batons

ice cubes

6–8 firm ripe tomatoes* [such as Ox Heart, heritage or Roma], peeled and cut into 1cm dice

sea salt flakes

6–9 grilled preserved artichokes, drained, dried with paper towel and cut into quarters

40ml extra virgin olive oil, plus extra for drizzling

aged balsamic vinegar, for drizzling

40 Ligurian olives, rinsed and dried with paper towel if stored in brine

freshly ground black pepper

2 handfuls torn basil leaves [green or purple or both]

½ × 47.5g can Ortiz* anchovy fillets, drained and dried with paper towel, then each cut into 2 pieces lengthwise

Serves 6

Tomato, Cucumber & Grilled Artichoke Salad

Make this salad during summer, when tomatoes are really full of flavour. Chilling the cucumbers provides a crisp contrast to the tomato. The sieved eggs enrich the salad while the anchovies and olives add saltiness. The sweet basil adds a finishing touch of freshness. Serve as an appetising entrée or to complement crumbed veal cutlets.

1 Prick the eggs with a pin at the widest end, then gently lower into a saucepan of simmering water and cook for 10 minutes. Remove and refresh under cold running water.

2 Toast the celery seeds in a dry frying pan until they smell fragrant.

3 Place the cucumber in a bowl of iced water. Leave for 20 minutes, then drain and dry each piece of cucumber well with paper towel. Transfer to a mixing bowl.

4 Place the tomato in a colander, sprinkle with salt and toss ever so gently, then leave to drain for 10–15 minutes. Pat dry with paper towel and add to the cucumber.

5 Add the artichokes to the bowl of cucumber and tomato, then moisten with olive oil and a dash of vinegar and add the olives, finishing with a few generous grinds of pepper and the celery seeds. Using your hands, gently combine the ingredients.

6 Distribute the salad among 6 deep entrée plates.

7 Shell the eggs, cut in half and push the yolks and whites separately through a coarse sieve into a bowl, then scatter over the salad.

8 Scatter with the basil and drizzle a thread of oil over. Crisscross the anchovy over the salad, then serve.

450g cooked dried or tinned chick peas, drained, skins pinched off

200g baby spinach, washed and spin-dried

2 handfuls finely shredded radicchio

12 grilled preserved artichokes, drained and cut into quarters

1 head fennel, top and bottom trimmed, finely shaved [reserve ¼ cup fennel fronds]

4 thin slices prosciutto, each cut into 3

½ clove garlic, any green shoot removed, finely chopped

3 anchovy fillets [preferably Ortiz* brand], drained and cut into small pieces

100ml extra virgin olive oil

20ml aged red-wine vinegar [such as Forum Cabernet vinegar*], or to taste

freshly ground black pepper

a pinch salt [optional]

2–3 tablespoons shredded flat-leaf parsley

Serves 4–6

Rustic Salad of Chick Peas, Prosciutto & Preserved Artichoke with Garlic & Anchovy Vinaigrette

Here is an entrée salad that could precede any simple main course. Its acidic, nutty and sweet flavours are balanced by the saltiness of the prosciutto and anchovies.

1 Place the chick peas, spinach, radicchio, artichokes, fennel and prosciutto in a suitably sized bowl.

2 Lightly mix the garlic, anchovy, olive oil, vinegar and pepper in a small bowl and taste for saltiness, adjusting as required [bearing in mind the saltiness of the anchovy and prosciutto]. Add the parsley and pour over the salad, then toss and serve.

1 large clove garlic, any green shoot removed	3 mustard fruit* figs, cut into small dice
60ml extra virgin olive oil	finely grated zest of 2 lemons
1 tablespoon lemon thyme leaves	**Vinaigrette**
6 quail, butterflied and patted dry	40ml hazelnut oil
300g wild rice	60ml grapeseed oil
1.25 litres water	20ml aged sherry vinegar
4–5 radicchio leaves, washed but not dried, rolled into a cigar shape, then shaved into 5mm-thick ribbons	20ml lime juice
120g Portobello mushrooms, stalks discarded, caps thinly sliced	1 tablespoon lemon thyme leaves
40ml verjuice*	sea salt and freshly ground white pepper
sea salt and freshly ground white pepper	**Serves 6**

Wild Rice & Roast Quail Salad

The delicate gaminess of the quail sits very well with the wild rice, while a contrast is offered by sweet mustard fruit, slightly bitter radicchio and a hint of aromatic lemon zest. Serve this delicious nutty-flavoured salad as an entrée before a main course of baked whole tropical fish or roast barramundi fillets.

1 Combine the garlic, olive oil and lemon thyme leaves and leave at room temperature for 30 minutes. Strain, then gently rub the quail all over with the scented oil and leave at room temperature until the rice is cooked.

2 Put the wild rice into a 3-litre capacity saucepan with the cold water and 1 teaspoon salt. Bring to the boil, then simmer over low heat for 40 minutes. The rice may burst if the temperature is too high so keep an eye on it.

3 To make the vinaigrette, whisk the ingredients together, then taste and adjust the seasoning.

4 Put the radicchio, mushrooms and verjuice in a saucepan, season lightly with salt and pepper, then cover and sweat over low heat for 5 minutes, stirring once or twice until softened.

5 Drain the wild rice well in a colander, then transfer to a large mixing bowl. Add two-thirds of the vinaigrette and the radicchio, mushrooms, mustard fruit figs and lemon zest. Season to taste, then fold the ingredients together. Cover with plastic film to keep warm while the quail is cooked.

6 Heat a cast-iron chargrill then season the quail and grill for 2–3 minutes, skin-side down. Flip the quail over and cook for another minute; they should be on the rare side.

7 Slice off the quail legs and put aside for the moment. Turn the quail over and pull out any remaining bones, then thinly slice the breasts on the diagonal, moistening them with the remaining vinaigrette. Fold the quail and vinaigrette into the wild rice with any juices that collected as they were carved.

8 Turn the rice salad onto a platter and garnish with the quail legs. Serve while still warm.

1 large red pepper

6–8 Ox Heart, heritage or vine-ripened tomatoes*

sea salt

20 basil leaves, gently torn into small pieces

freshly ground black pepper

best quality extra virgin olive oil, for drizzling

1 large Lebanese cucumber, peeled

2 × 210g jars Ortiz tuna* fillets or 2 × 300g jars Crespi tuna,* drained

aged balsamic vinegar, for drizzling

30 small black olives [such as Ligurian]

¼ cup small salted capers, soaked in warm water, drained and dried

Serves 6

A Simple Tuna Salad

Bottled and tinned tuna fillets are often considered inferior to the fresh product; however, brands such as Spanish Ortiz and Italian Crespi tinned tuna* are really superior to supermarket versions. They are better in this type of salad than their fresh counterpart as the preserved tuna is very moist and will absorb the flavour of the other ingredients more readily. This quickly prepared salad needs nothing more than good bread to make a very pleasant entrée in summer.

1   Grill the pepper over a gas flame or on a cast-iron chargrill until blackened. Transfer to a plate and seal with plastic film, then leave for 15 minutes. Peel off the skin with your fingertips and with the aid of a paring knife. Don't be tempted to wash the skin since this will spoil the flavour. Slice off the tops and bottoms, then cut in half lengthwise. Remove any seeds and membrane, then cut into very thin matchsticks and cut in half.

2   Cut the tomatoes into 8mm-thick slices and lay them, without overlapping, in a wide colander placed over a bowl. Sprinkle with salt and leave for 15 minutes; the flavour will improve. This gives the salad a special quality.

3   Pat the tomato slices dry with paper towel and distribute between 6 flat entrée plates, arranging the slices in 2 overlapping lines. Scatter with half the basil. Grind some pepper on top and moisten generously with olive oil.

4   Cut the cucumber into paper-thin slices, preferably using a mandoline.*

5   Scatter the tomato with the peppers and cucumber, then distribute the tuna evenly between the plates. Moisten with more olive oil and a very little balsamic vinegar. Finish with the olives, capers and remaining basil.

1kg mixed tomatoes,* stalks removed

sea salt flakes and freshly ground black pepper

extra virgin olive oil, for drizzling

Banyuls,* for drizzling

about 30 mixed olives, of various colours and varieties

2 Lebanese cucumbers

Serves 6

Mixed Tomato Salad with Olives & Cucumber

This simple salad calls for several tomato varieties with contrasting flavours, textures and colours; fortunately, there are plenty to choose from these days. I have mentioned the Love Bite tomatoes* in other recipes; they have a particularly firm texture and a great flavour. The little yellow grape tomatoes add a sweet touch, while teardrops offer lots of flavour with slight acidity. Ox Hearts are also full of flavour but be sure they are quite firm since they tend to go mushy once salted if they are too ripe. Black Russians, also known as Kumatoes, are dark green until they ripen to a greenish-black; I use the greener ones that are beginning to soften for the colour they bring to this special yet simple dish. Salting the tomatoes is an old technique from Nice and helps to develop a fuller flavour, although go easy with this lest the salad be too salty. Good bread is a must with this salad.

1   Rinse the tomatoes under cold running water and wipe dry. Slice the larger ones lengthwise into 1cm-thick slices; the smaller oval varieties may be halved lengthwise and the tiniest tomatoes halved crosswise. The aim is to make a feature of the different shapes and colours as well as provide a cut surface whereby the salt may penetrate the flesh.

2   Lay the larger slices on cake-cooling racks and place the smaller tomatoes in a colander. Scatter the salt very lightly over the tomato and leave to drain for 15 minutes. Pat dry with paper towel, very gently since the flesh will have softened considerably.

3   Arrange the tomato on a large platter, then grind over some pepper. Moisten generously with the olive oil and a very little vinegar, then scatter over the olives.

4   Cut the cucumbers into paper-thin slices, preferably using a mandoline,* then scatter over the tomatoes and serve.

Classic Salads

Salades classiques

300g smoked belly bacon	
150ml olive oil	
6 × 15mm-thick slices light sourdough bread	
1 clove garlic, bruised with the flat of a knife, peeled	
6 eggs, at fridge temperature	
1.5 litres water	
1 teaspoon white-wine vinegar	
200g frisée lettuce, washed and spin-dried, torn into smaller pieces if large	

Vinaigrette

3 eschalots, finely diced
60ml extra virgin olive oil
40ml walnut oil
20ml aged red-wine vinegar [such as Banyuls*]
sea salt and freshly ground black pepper

Serves 6

Salade Frisée Lardons

This is probably the most common entrée found on bistro and brasserie menus all over France. The slightly bitter frisée leaves are anointed with a sharp vinaigrette flavoured with eschalots and the runny yolk of a soft-poached egg. Little batons of cured pork belly are fried to provide saltiness, while fried croûtons bring the flavour and texture of this salad to perfection. Since this cured pork belly is unavailable in Australia, the best substitute is smoked belly bacon. If you are concerned about poaching eggs then look for specially designed 'poaching boats' made by Claystone Pottery* as they make poaching much more successful. A wonderful dish to begin any meal.

1 Preheat the oven to 80°C. Cut the skin off the belly bacon, then cut into lardons about 1cm × 3cm. Heat 1 teaspoon of the olive oil in a small frying pan and fry the lardons until slightly crisp. Drain on paper towel and keep warm in the oven.

2 To make the croûtons, cut 5cm rounds from of the slices of bread and lightly shallow-fry them in the remaining olive oil. Drain, dry on paper towel and then rub with the garlic.

3 Prepare a bowl of iced water and set aside. Break 2 of the eggs at a time into small cups or little bowls [this helps the eggs to keep their rounded shape as they cook]. In a large saucepan, bring the water and vinegar to the boil and poach the eggs so that the yolks are still soft and runny, about 2½ minutes. Remove with a slotted spoon and plunge immediately into the iced water. Drain on a clean tea towel. This can be done an hour in advance if desired but cover the eggs with plastic film.

4 To make the vinaigrette, whisk all the ingredients together, then taste for seasoning and adjust if desired.

5 To serve, toss the frisée with some of the vinaigrette and arrange in shallow entrée-sized bowls. Scatter with the lardons, then top with a poached egg on a croûton. Drizzle over a little more vinaigrette and serve immediately.

150g celeriac, cut into 1cm dice

100g pale inner stalks celery, washed and cut into 1cm dice

2–3 eating apples [such as Gala]

juice of 1 lemon

120–150ml very thick Mayonnaise*

150g walnut kernels

6 small inner or baby cos lettuce leaves, washed and spin-dried

2 punnets mustard cress or 1 very large handful watercress sprigs

Serves 6 as an accompaniment

Waldorf Salad

This salad is very popular in the United States, where it was created by the chef of the Waldorf–Astoria Hotel in New York in the 1890s. Recipes vary dramatically in the proportions of ingredients called for so it is difficult to know what the original recipe was really like.

The success of this salad relies upon using the freshest walnuts as they tend to turn rancid very easily. I suggest you begin by sourcing the best quality nuts before considering making a Waldorf salad. It is also important that the nuts are peeled. This may sound like too much trouble but the difference is remarkable, since the absence of skin releases their sweet flavour.

The addition of lettuce makes this version lighter and fresher. If time permits, you might like to add peeled seedless grapes as they were often included in older recipes.

1 Blanch the celeriac in a saucepan of boiling salted water for 2 minutes, then refresh under cold running water and drain well.

2 Combine the celeriac and celery in a mixing bowl. Peel and core the apples, then cut into 1cm dice; you need 250g. Toss well with a little lemon juice to prevent discolouration. Drain briefly in a colander, then pat dry with a clean cloth or paper towel. Add to the celeriac and celery.

3 Mix in a little of the mayonnaise initially to ensure that the finished texture is not too wet.

4 Drop the walnuts into a pan of boiling water and allow to come back to the boil, then drain. Using a small paring knife, remove as much of the skin as possible, then chop each into 5–6 pieces. Fold into the salad.

5 Distribute the salad between the cos leaves and garnish with the snipped cress or watercress sprigs, then serve.

500g Savoy cabbage, core removed, finely shredded

150g celeriac, cut into fine julienne

1 large carrot, finely shredded

1 small eschalot, very finely sliced

1 red pepper, top sliced off and membrane and seeds discarded, finely sliced

1 × 47.5g tin Ortiz* anchovy fillets, drained, dried and roughly chopped

1 handful flat-leaf parsley, washed and shredded

2 eggs, at fridge temperature

sea salt and freshly ground white pepper

1 heaped teaspoon Dijon mustard

150–200ml olive oil

tarragon vinegar or white-wine vinegar, to taste

Serves 6 as an accompaniment

Coleslaw with a Twist

Here is a variation on the traditional salad that is lovely with a barbecue of sausages and perhaps lamb chump chops marinated in olive oil with rosemary.

1 Assemble the cabbage, celeriac, carrot, eschalot, pepper, anchovy and parsley in a bowl large enough to toss the ingredients easily.

2 Prick the eggs with a pin at their widest end. Lower gently into boiling water and cook for 3 minutes. Crack each egg over a small bowl and let the yolk fall into the bowl. Season lightly with salt and pepper, then whisk in the mustard. Slowly whisk in the oil to thicken the vinaigrette. Acidulate with vinegar to a slightly sharp taste, then adjust the seasoning with salt and pepper. Chop the eggwhite into small pieces and stir into the vinaigrette.

3 Moisten the vegetables with two-thirds of the vinaigrette and leave for 30 minutes; as they may produce their own moisture it is best to check the texture before adding more vinaigrette before serving.

4 Add more vinaigrette if required. Turn into a salad bowl and serve.

1 large or 2 smaller pears, ripe but on the firm side, washed and dried

juice of ½ lemon

4 handfuls small watercress sprigs, washed and spin-dried

4 radicchio leaves, washed and spin-dried, sliced into 5mm ribbons

6 baby cos lettuce leaves, washed and spin-dried

1 bunch chives, cut into 2cm lengths [optional]

Avocado vinaigrette

1 ripe avocado,* on the soft side [so that it will purée easily]

juice of ½ lime, or to taste

sea salt and freshly ground white pepper

2 teaspoons walnut oil

20ml light sour cream, stirred until smooth if firm

½–1 teaspoon sweet paprika

Serves 6 as an accompaniment

Salad of Watercress, Radicchio & Sliced Pear with Avocado Vinaigrette

This little salad is composed of contrasting flavours, textures and colours. It would be a good accompaniment to crumbed lamb cutlets, Vienna schnitzel or grilled salmon fillets served with lemon wedges. If you like, add some bitter leaves such as dandelion or witlof to give the salad extra zing.

1   Cut the pear in half lengthwise. Remove the core with a parisienne cutter,* then slice very thinly directly into a bowl with the lemon juice. Toss gently, then drain in a sieve.

2   To make the avocado vinaigrette, cut the avocado in half, peel and roughly dice. Transfer to a blender or food processor with the lime juice. Lightly season, then purée until smooth. Add the walnut oil and process briefly. Transfer to a small bowl, then stir in the sour cream and paprika. If the consistency is too thick, whisk in a little cold water.

3   Put the vinaigrette into a large mixing bowl, then add the leaves and pear and toss gently with your hands. Serve in a salad bowl, scattered with chives, if using.

1 large potato [about 200g], cut into 15mm dice	150g cornichons,* cut into 5mm-thick slices
1 celeriac, cut into 15mm dice [to yield about 200g]	freshly ground white pepper
sea salt	2 tablespoons salted capers, soaked briefly in warm water, then rinsed and dried with paper towel
1 large carrot [about 200g], cut into 15mm dice	**Mayonnaise**
150g podded fresh peas [frozen peas can be used]	2 egg yolks
150g baby beans, cut into 2cm lengths	2 teaspoons Dijon mustard
6 eggs, at fridge temperature	¼ teaspoon sea salt
100g button mushrooms, stalks removed, caps sliced	freshly ground white pepper
1 head baby fennel, trimmed and very finely diced [to yield about 150g]	100ml extra virgin olive oil
	100ml vegetable oil
2 tomatoes, peeled, seeded and cut into 15mm dice [to yield about 200g]	aged white-wine vinegar [such as Forum Chardonnay vinegar*], to taste
900g picked crabmeat, carefully checked for any trace of shell	finely grated zest of 1 lemon
	tiniest pinch cayenne pepper, or to taste
2 tablespoons snipped tarragon	**Serves 10–12**
½ cup finely shredded flat-leaf parsley	

Salade Russe

While researching this book I believe I came across more variations for this recipe than for any other. Many classic recipes include lobster, truffles and caviar, but one element that remains constant is the inclusion of an assortment of vegetables. This is a version we made for a Melbourne Cup Day lunch as a set-menu entrée for 160 guests; I seem to remember two of us chopping and cooking vegetables for hours on end! Serve as an entrée at any time, although it is particularly good for a buffet. Simply halve the quantities for six entrée portions.

1   To make the mayonnaise, whisk the egg yolks, mustard, salt and a generous amount of pepper in a mixing bowl. Slowly add the combined oils in a fine stream, whisking continuously and taking care not to add more oil before the previous addition is absorbed. Continue adding the remaining oil until quite thick, then acidulate with a little vinegar and season to taste. The texture should be thick enough to coat the salad ingredients. Finish with the lemon zest and cayenne. Cover closely with plastic film and leave at room temperature until required.

2   Steam the potato over boiling water for 12 minutes or until tender. Leave to cool.

3   Cook the celeriac in a saucepan of boiling salted water for 8 minutes or until tender. Drain or remove with a slotted spoon, then leave to cool.

4   Cook the carrot in a saucepan of boiling salted water for 8 minutes or until tender. Drain or remove with a slotted spoon, then leave to cool.

5   Cook the peas in a saucepan of boiling salted water for 5 minutes or until tender. Drain or remove with a slotted spoon, then leave to cool.

6   Cook the beans in a saucepan of boiling salted water for 4 minutes or until tender. Drain or remove with a slotted spoon, then leave to cool.

7   Prick the eggs with a pin, then cook in a saucepan of boiling water for 10 minutes. Cool under cold running water until cold, then shell and slice.

8   Put half the mayonnaise in a large bowl, then add the cooked and raw vegetables, crab, tarragon, parsley and cornichons. Season lightly and, using food-grade gloved hands, gently fold the ingredients together, adding more mayonnaise so that everything is just coated and not at all sloppy in texture. Refrigerate for at least 30 minutes to allow the flavours to mingle.

9   Transfer to a wide shallow serving bowl or individual deep entrée plates, then arrange the egg on top, finishing with capers. Serve at once.

| 3–4 carrots [about 250g], peeled |
| 1 small eschalot, very finely diced |
| extra virgin olive oil, for drizzling |
| fine sea salt and freshly ground white pepper |
| 2 teaspoons lemon juice, or to taste |
| **Serves 4** |

Raw Grated Carrot Salad
Carottes Rapées

This traditional carrot salad is available in every charcuterie and *traiteur* [takeaway food store] throughout France, along with huge bowls of celeriac bound in a mustard-flavoured mayonnaise known as *rémoulade*. The carrots should be young and sweet and grated in fine longish threads. The old-fashioned Mouli-julienne* rotary cutter makes the best grated carrots but the vegetable-cutting attachments of food processors also do a fine job. Failing these, use a hand-held upright grater and shred the carrots in fine long threads, keeping the carrot at a close angle to the grater. If using older carrots don't include the hard cores.

I have included a few variations to this classic dish to be served as part of an hors d'oeuvre entrée. The spicy heat of the large white radish called daikon adds an interesting twist to the classic salad. To make grated carrots and daikon, follow the method below, using a ratio of about one-third daikon to two-thirds carrot for a good balance of flavours.

1 Grate the carrots, then add the eschalot and moisten with a little olive oil. Season to taste, then acidulate initially with a little of the lemon juice, adding more to freshen and develop the flavour; avoid making the mixture too wet. Cover with plastic film and refrigerate for 20–30 minutes to allow the flavours to mingle.

Grated Carrot and Fennel with Toasted Fennel Seed

Take a small head of fennel, then cut into quarters lengthwise and shave thinly with a sharp knife or a mandoline,* then toss well with extra virgin olive oil and lemon juice. Toast 2 teaspoons fennel seeds in a dry frying pan over medium heat for a minute or so until they smell aromatic. When they have cooled, grind to a powder using a mortar and pestle or spice grinder and transfer to a small sieve, then dust over the salad just before serving. For a spike of saltiness, try shaving thin slices of Pecorino Romano over the salad.

3–4 eggs, at fridge temperature

8 tomatoes, cored, cut into 2cm-thick slices

sea salt

1 clove garlic, smashed

2 green peppers, cut into thin matchsticks

4 spring onions, white part only, trimmed and sliced on the diagonal

2 small Lebanese cucumbers, peeled [optional] and very finely sliced

120g small black olives, rinsed and dried with paper towel

torn lettuce [such as cos or red oak-leaf], washed and spin-dried [optional]

250–300g tuna* in oil [preferably Ortiz red label or Crespi], drained well

10 anchovy fillets [preferably Ortiz* brand], drained well, cut lengthwise into 2–3 pieces

12 basil leaves

Vinaigrette

120ml best quality extra virgin olive oil

sea salt and freshly ground black pepper

2 teaspoons tarragon vinegar or Banyuls,* or to taste

Serves 6

Salade Niçoise

Salade niçoise shares the same propensity for misinterpretation as Caesar salad – one rarely sees the original version outside Nice, and even there I have encountered some real hotchpotches. There should never be any cooked vegetables used since it is actually an hors d'oeuvre based on what the French call *crudités* or raw vegetables. Given the cost of fresh tuna, anchovies were traditionally used by the locals. If you want to use tuna it most certainly should not be fresh. Purchase the best quality bottled or tinned varieties. The ingredients need to be coated with flakes of tuna, fragments of hard-boiled egg and the dressing, which correctly should not contain vinegar. This is a matter of taste so I tend to make a richer vinaigrette using a touch of tarragon vinegar.

The soul of a great salade niçoise is, of course, using the best flavoured tomatoes available. The old niçois folk salted firm tomatoes before they began preparing the other vegetables. This technique develops the full flavour but has the disadvantage of rendering the tomatoes on the soft side and not looking really fresh, although the flavour is so much better. While the other vegetables chosen may vary with what is in season there are a few essentials such as green peppers, cucumbers and black olives. Sliced raw globe artichoke hearts and very tiny raw podded broad beans may be included when available. As to using lettuce, again this is not traditional so it is up to individual taste. Very small or torn cos leaves provide some texture and torn red oak-leaf lettuce adds some colour.

This salad is best presented on a deep platter so leave adding the dressing and tossing until your beautiful salade niçoise is on the table. I adore this dish as the colours and aroma transport me to the sunny shores of southern France.

1 Prick the eggs with a pin, then cook in a saucepan of boiling water for 10 minutes. Refresh under cold running water until cold. Shell and cut into quarters.

2 Place the tomato in a colander, then sprinkle with sea salt. Leave for 15–20 minutes, then gently pat dry with paper towel.

3 Rub a platter with the garlic and season it lightly. Arrange the tomato, pepper, spring onion, cucumber, olives, lettuce [if using], egg, flaked tuna and anchovies on the platter so that the various colours contrast with each other. Gently tear the basil and scatter over the salad.

4 To make the vinaigrette, mix the ingredients, adding enough salt, pepper and vinegar to your taste, and distribute evenly over the salad. Toss gently so that the ingredients are anointed evenly.

The Very Best Tomato &
Mozzarella Salad by Steve Manfredi

Getting away from my restaurants was essential so that I could write this book in peace and quiet. I ventured to the Central Coast of New South Wales to stay at the Bells at Killcare resort, where my colleague and old friend Steve Manfredi has established a fine kitchen serving his delicious Italian food. Steve is growing a wide variety of tomatoes, one of which, the Costoluto Fiorentino, comes into its own when gently roasted. The salad was so good I ordered it three times during my stay in this superb resort. Here is the recipe in Steve's words.

First take as many tomatoes as you have people. Simple enough, but the best tomato for this dish is the one you've grown yourself. At Bells we've been very fortunate as cooks. We have had the room and the will to establish a kitchen garden. It's been so successful that we're planning to more than double it.

The tomato we use for this dish is an old Italian variety, the Costoluto Fiorentino, an heirloom ribbed tomato from Florence. Seeds for this can be ordered from **theitaliangardener.com.au**. Large truss tomatoes can be substituted while you wait for yours to grow.

Take a sharp knife and remove the woody part of the tomato at the top where the stem was. Cut into the flesh to create a 2cm cavity. Place the tomatoes on a baking tray and preheat the oven to 180°C. Pour as much extra virgin olive oil into the cavity as it will hold without overflowing. Season with salt and pepper and roast for 10–15 minutes or until the tomato has softened and is tender without having split. Remove and set aside.

In a mortar, place 2 good handfuls fresh basil leaves, 60g pine nuts, 2 medium-sized peeled cloves garlic and a good pinch coarse sea salt. Pound until everything has broken down to a paste. Add enough extra virgin olive oil, mixing, to give the desired consistency. Mix in ½–⅔ cup grated Parmigiano Reggiano and adjust the seasoning.

We start to assemble the dish with a bed of a thinly sliced witlof on each plate from the Bells garden called Pan di Zucchero. It heads up like a large cos lettuce but is tighter and has a more interesting flavour, sweet with a hint of bitterness. Seeds for this can also be found at the same website. A slice of buffalo mozzarella is placed on top and then the roast tomato. Finish by drizzling plenty of pesto over the dish and serve. If the pesto is too thick, dilute with a little water to a drizzling consistency.

3 small blood oranges or 2 navel oranges

3–4 heads baby fennel, tops and bottoms trimmed [reserve ¼ cup of the fronds], roughly chopped

30 black olives [such as Ligurian]

extra virgin olive oil, for drizzling

sea salt and freshly ground black pepper

100–120g parmesan [preferably aged Parmigiano Reggiano]

1 good handful rocket sprigs [optional], coarse stalks removed

Serves 6 as an entrée

Fennel, Orange & Olive Salad

The marriage of these ingredients is a mainstay of the Italian kitchen. Generally moistened with extra virgin olive oil and a little vinegar [and sometimes orange juice], the result is a refreshing and cleansing salad, that is a lovely match for rich meats such as pork or hand-crafted sausages [see opposite].

Traditionally, the orange zest and pith are removed using a sharp knife following the contour of the fruit. The fruit is then sliced across the width of the orange. The fennel is sliced quite finely and the two are tossed with oil, adding a dash of red-wine vinegar, black olives and a little pepper. Here is a variation of a more substantial nature as an offering to begin a meal. This salad calls for the best Tuscan extra virgin olive oil.

1 Using a very sharp paring knife, cut a thin slice crosswise from the top and bottom of the oranges. Place a cut surface on a board and allow the knife to follow the contour of the fruit between the flesh and pith; just take your time and aim for a smoothly rounded finish. Now hold the orange in one hand over a strainer set on a bowl so as to collect the fruit and juice. Slice between the pith and flesh to produce fillets that will fall into the strainer below. This may be done ahead of time. Reserve the collected juice.

2 Ideally, just before serving, using a mandoline* or very sharp chef's knife, shave the fennel into 3mm-thick slices, then put in a serving bowl or distribute between 6 flat entrée plates. Scatter with the reserved fronds, the olives and orange fillets.

3 Moisten with a good drizzle of oil, about 2 teaspoons of reserved blood orange juice, a touch of salt and a few grinds of pepper.

4 Use a vegetable peeler or mandoline* to shave parmesan on top, scatter with the rocket [if using], then serve.

1.5kg veal loin fillet, removed from the fridge 1 hour before cooking

1 × 47.5g can anchovy fillets [preferably Ortiz*], drained and cut into 4 pieces each

sea salt and freshly ground white pepper

extra virgin olive oil, for cooking

250 ml water

120ml veal stock or chicken stock or water

Tuna sauce

4 eggs, at fridge temperature

sea salt and freshly ground white pepper

200ml extra virgin olive oil

2 × 210g cans tuna* in oil [preferably Ortiz brand] or 2 × 300g cans tuna* in oil [preferably Crespi brand], drained and flaked

juice of 1–2 lemons

Salad

3–4 witlof, outer leaves discarded

1 cup flat-leaf parsley leaves, washed and spin-dried, torn into smaller pieces

2 handfuls small watercress sprigs, washed and spin-dried

4 large Ox Heart tomatoes* or 6 Love Bite or truss tomatoes,* cores removed

180g Ligurian olives, rinsed and dried with paper towel

¼–⅓ cup salted capers, soaked in warm water, then rinsed and dried with paper towel

1 × 47.5g can anchovy fillets [preferably Ortiz* brand], drained and halved lengthwise

60g parmesan [preferably Parmigiano Reggiano], thinly shaved

Serves 6–8

Vitello Tonnato Salad

Vitello tonnato is a classic dish from the Italian kitchen and just about everyone loves it. Traditionally, the eye of the silverside [*girello*] is poached but this cut can become rather dry if overcooked. The cold veal is thinly sliced and coated with a tuna-based mayonnaise, often enriched with anchovies and capers, then refrigerated for several hours or overnight. In researching the recipe I discovered many variations to the tuna sauce and found that, in some cases, roasted veal loin or rump replaces the traditional cut and cooking method. Here is a lovely salad to serve for an al fresco summer lunch.

1   Preheat the oven to 160°C. Using a thin paring knife, make 16 deep incisions over the surface of the veal. Insert an anchovy piece into each incision, pushing them into the meat. Wipe the veal dry with paper towel if it is moist, then season with salt, pepper and olive oil, rubbing the surface to coat it with the seasoning.

2   Heat 20ml or more of oil in a roasting pan or large ovenproof frying pan until very hot, then seal the veal on all the surfaces. Discard the oil and put a cake-cooling rack into the pan, then place the veal on top. Add the water to the pan and roast for 30–40 minutes, topping up with extra water if necessary. The veal should feel springy to the touch and be very slightly pink inside; to be sure it is sufficiently cooked insert a thin knife, which should reveal slightly pink juices. Transfer the veal to a plate to cool, then refrigerate for about 1 hour or until firm enough to carve thinly. Remove the rack from the pan, then add the stock or water, place over high heat and reduce to 40ml. Strain into a small bowl to cool and set aside.

3   To make the sauce, prick the eggs with a fine pin, then plunge into a saucepan of boiling water. Cook 2 of the eggs for 3 minutes and the remaining 2 for 8 minutes. Refresh the 8-minute eggs under cold running water.

4   Crack the 3-minute eggs over a bowl and use a teaspoon to scoop out the yolks. The whites are not required. Whisk in ¼ teaspoon salt and some pepper, then slowly whisk in the oil to make a thickened dressing.

5   Shell and roughly chop the 8-minute eggs and transfer to a food processor with the tuna. Process to a smooth paste then, with the motor running, add the 40ml reduced stock and the dressing then pulse to emulsify. Season with lemon juice and taste, correcting the salt and pepper. The consistency should be thick enough to coat the sliced veal, but if it is too thick dilute with a little cold water. Transfer to a shallow wide bowl.

6   For the salad, cut each witlof lengthwise into 6 pieces and distribute over a platter. Combine the parsley and watercress and scatter over the platter. Cut the tomatoes roughly into 15mm chunks and scatter over the platter with the olives and capers.

7   Carve the veal quite thinly using a very sharp knife. Dip or coat the veal in the sauce, then lay on the salad, folding each slice in half. Dilute any remaining sauce with a little more lemon juice or water and drizzle over the vegetables. Decorate the veal with the anchovy fillets and finish with the parmesan.

3 handfuls mixed salad leaves [such as baby cos, red oak-leaf, witlof, radicchio and butter lettuce], washed and spin-dried [except the witlof]

Aïoli

2 cloves garlic, any green shoot removed, finely chopped

sea salt and freshly ground white pepper

1 egg yolk

1 teaspoon Dijon mustard

40–50ml extra virgin olive oil

40–50ml grapeseed oil

lemon juice, to taste

Dressing

80ml Aïoli [see opposite]

30ml sour cream

1 tablespoon finely chopped flat-leaf parsley

1 tablespoon chopped dill

1 tablespoon finely chopped chives

1½ tablespoons drained and chopped anchovies

sea salt and freshly ground white pepper

tiniest pinch cayenne pepper

lemon juice, to taste

Serves 4

Green Goddess Salad

1   The dressing needs a little time to mature so start by making the aïoli. Work the garlic to a paste with a pinch of salt on a chopping board, then transfer to a small mixing bowl with the egg yolk and mustard. Whisk until smooth, then work in the combined oils very slowly at first, making sure the previous addition is emulsified before adding more. Finish with a little lemon juice and correct the seasoning. Only 80ml will be required [the remainder will keep closely covered with plastic film in the fridge for up to 2 days and is delicious with fried calamari].

2   For the dressing, whisk 80ml of the aïoli with the sour cream, herbs and anchovies, then season to taste with salt, pepper, cayenne and lemon juice; the consistency should be that of thick pouring cream.

3   Tear the larger leaves into small pieces.

4   Put half the dressing into a large mixing bowl, add the leaves then drizzle over the remaining dressing. Toss with your hands, then distribute between 6 small bowls.

Salads at Pavilion on the Park

Our table d'hôte dinner menu throughout the late 1970s consisted of seven courses, namely crudités, a choice of two entrées, soup, sorbet, choice of two main courses, a composed salad, then a dessert. The salads were served in small Japanese lacquer bowls, black on the outside and deep-red inside. We sourced many of these salads from the broad American repertoire, where they play an important role as starters. The Green Goddess Salad, Florida Salad overleaf and Salade Mimosa on page 74 are a few that were popular with our guests.

1 orange	**Dressing**
½ grapefruit [the pink variety if available]	1 small clove garlic, smashed
1 small avocado*	60ml extra virgin olive oil
1 baby cos, small inner leaves only, washed and spin-dried	2 teaspoons grapefruit juice [reserved from filleting]
1 handful small rocket sprigs, washed and spin-dried	1–2 teaspoons aged white-wine vinegar [such as Forum Chardonnay vinegar*]
2 handfuls small watercress sprigs, washed and spin-dried	sea salt and freshly ground white pepper
1–2 handfuls mignonette leaves, washed and spin-dried, torn into small pieces	**Serves 6**
¼ cup chopped dill	

Florida Salad

1 To make the dressing, rub a small bowl with the garlic, then discard the debris. Whisk together the oil, grapefruit juice and vinegar, then season with salt and pepper to taste and check the seasoning.

2 Using a very sharp paring knife, cut a thin slice crosswise from the top and bottom of the orange. Place a cut surface on a chopping board and allow the knife to follow the contour of the fruit between the flesh and pith; just take your time and aim for a smoothly rounded finish. Now hold the orange in one hand over a strainer set on a bowl so as to collect the fruit and juice. Slice between the flesh and pith to produce fillets that will fall into the strainer. This may be done ahead of time. Repeat with the grapefruit, retaining 2 teaspoons of juice for the dressing. Drain well before the next step.

3 Only two-thirds of the orange fillets and half the grapefruit will be required; cut each grapefruit fillet into 3 pieces.

4 Cut the avocado in half lengthwise and gently twist to separate the halves. Hold the half with the stone still attached in one hand; tap the stone with a sharp knife, then twist the knife and the stone will be released. Peel the avocado and place on a chopping board. Cut each half in 2 lengthwise, then cover with plastic film, pressing it against the fruit.

5 Select only the small inner leaves of the cos; should more be needed then tear the larger leaves into small pieces.

6 Place all the leaves in a large mixing bowl, scatter with the orange and grapefruit, then moisten with some of the vinaigrette. Toss using your hands, then arrange in 6 small bowls.

7 Cut the avocado into 5mm-thick slices and distribute between the salads, finishing with a little more vinaigrette. Scatter with the dill and serve.

3 eggs, at fridge temperature

2 small oranges [preferably the blood variety], filleted*

1 cup torn dandelion leaves, washed and spin-dried

2 handfuls baby rocket, washed and spin-dried

2 handfuls watercress sprigs, washed and spin-dried

6 witlof leaves

Vinaigrette

1 teaspoon English mustard or 2 teaspoons Dijon mustard with a tiny pinch cayenne pepper

60ml extra virgin olive oil

20ml cider vinegar* or aged sherry vinegar

sea salt and freshly ground white pepper

Serves 6

Salade Mimosa

Mimosa refers to a French garnish consisting of separately sieved hard-boiled eggwhite and yolks, which is thought to be reminiscent of the yellow and white flowers of the acacia tree, hence the name. A coarse sieve is essential to achieve the powdery texture that makes this salad special. The orange fillets play a contrasting role to refresh the rich flavour of this salad. Serve after a roasted game or pork dish.

1 Use a pin to prick the eggs, then lower them into boiling water and cook for 10 minutes. Drain and refresh under cold running water, then shell them. Cut the eggs in half lengthwise and separate the yolks from the whites. Use a wooden spoon to press the eggwhites through a coarse sieve first, then follow with the yolks.

2 Drain the orange fillets well.

3 To make the vinaigrette, whisk the ingredients together thoroughly and check the seasoning.

4 Place the leaves in a large mixing bowl, moisten with the vinaigrette and toss with your hands, then distribute between 6 small bowls. Add the orange fillets and the egg mimosa, then serve.

250–300g Italian-style bread [such as ciabatta], crusts removed

1kg ripe tomatoes* [such as Love Bites, Romas, Ox Hearts or Black Russians], cored and cut into 2cm pieces

1 red onion, thinly sliced

2 large cloves garlic, any green shoot removed, roughly chopped

120g small black olives [such as Ligurian or the tiny wild Australian variety]

1 large Lebanese cucumber, cut into 3mm-thick slices

1 bunch basil, leaves picked, large leaves gently torn into smaller pieces

sea salt

80–100ml extra virgin olive oil

20–40ml aged red-wine vinegar [such as Forum Cabernet vinegar*]

freshly ground black pepper

Serves 4–6

Bread & Tomato Salad

This Tuscan dish is called *panzanella* and is correctly made with a type of bread from that region that is made without salt. The bread has a firm crust, fine texture and is very white. It becomes stale and unpalatable after a day or two, making it ideal to use up in this simple peasant salad. A good substitute is ciabatta, but both breads are readily available at Italian food stores. While it should be made from either of the breads I've mentioned to be authentic, as the aim is to use up stale bread you'll find that sourdough is an excellent alternative provided it is moistened with water and not vinegar. Traditionally the bread is moistened with water and sometimes vinegar, then combined with full-flavoured tomatoes, garlic, basil and olives. That said I am sure every Tuscan cook has their own preferences for the flavouring ingredients, which can include capers, celery, onions and so on. Clearly, this is a salad for summer, a time when one can rely on the availability of really good tomatoes, which make a *panzanella* delicious. Serve it as an entrée before barbecued fish and a leaf salad.

1   Roughly tear the bread into 3cm pieces, then put in a large mixing bowl and gradually moisten with water [or vinegar], using a sprinkling action and tossing constantly to distribute the water evenly. Leave for 10 minutes.

2   Place the bread, tomato, onion, garlic, olives, cucumber and basil in a bowl. Sprinkle lightly with salt, tossing at the same time with the oil and a little vinegar until the tomato looks glazed with oil. Add the pepper.

3   Transfer to a platter or large salad bowl and leave for 10 minutes for the flavours to develop before serving.

Main Course Salads

Salades en plat principal

1 × 1kg piece corned silverside	**Mayonnaise**
1 large onion, peeled	2 egg yolks
3 cloves	1 heaped teaspoon English mustard
2 carrots, roughly chopped	¼ teaspoon sea salt, or to taste
1 stalk celery, roughly chopped	freshly ground black pepper
bouquet garni* [2 bay leaves, 6 parsley stalks, 4 sprigs thyme, 2–3 strips lemon zest and 10 lightly crushed black peppercorns all wrapped in a muslin cloth and tied with kitchen twine]	150ml grapeseed oil
	100ml extra virgin olive oil
	aged white-wine vinegar, to taste
Salad	5 tablespoons finely chopped curly-leaf parsley
200g Savoy cabbage, core removed, shaved very thinly	**Serves 6**
1 large carrot, grated [to yield 200g]	
1 small red onion, finely shaved	
Halen Môn pure sea salt*	
2 tablespoons small salted capers, soaked in warm water, rinsed and dried with paper towel	
6–8 small dill-pickled cucumbers	

Corned Beef Salad

I have fond memories of my mother's corned beef, which she served during the colder months as a Sunday lunch. Tradition dictated that the evening meal would consist of the leftovers with a salad of tomatoes, beetroot and possibly some cucumber, dressed with a creamy dressing based on Carnation condensed milk. Playing with this idea I thought of this salad as an excellent dish for a casual wintertime lunch. Follow with an old-fashioned dessert such as a baked custard or trifle. A retro menu perhaps, but enjoyable nonetheless.

1 Place the silverside in a large saucepan and cover with cold water. Bring to the boil, then remove the silverside and rinse under cold running water. Discard the water and wash the pan. Return the silverside to the clean pan, then add the onion studded with cloves, carrot, celery and bouquet garni and cover generously with cold water.

2 Bring to the boil, then skim the surface well. Simmer over medium heat for 1½–2 hours or until tender, skimming the surface and topping up with extra water as necessary; the silverside must be immersed at all times. Transfer the silverside to a platter and leave to cool at room temperature, then wrap in plastic film and refrigerate until needed.

3 To make the mayonnaise, whisk the egg yolks, mustard, salt and a generous amount of pepper in a mixing bowl. Slowly add the combined oils in a fine stream, whisking continuously and taking care not to add more oil before the previous addition is absorbed. Continue adding the remaining oil until quite thick, then acidulate with vinegar and season to taste. The texture should be thick enough to coat the salad ingredients. Whisk in the parsley.

4 Trim away and discard any fat from the corned beef and cut into 5cm slices across the grain. Shred using your fingers along the natural grain of the meat into a mixing bowl large enough to hold all the ingredients.

5 To make the salad, add the cabbage, carrot and onion to the bowl, then combine with about half the mayonnaise to start, folding with a tablespoon. Add more mayonnaise as required to produce a bound but not sloppy texture, keeping in mind that the vegetables will produce moisture as they marinate; it is better to keep the texture on the dry side to start.

6 Transfer to a deep wide bowl then scatter with the smoked salt and capers. Serve the pickled cucumbers in a separate bowl since their role is to provide some crunchy freshness as a contrast to the creaminess of the salad.

2–2.5kg black mussels, cleaned

2 cloves garlic, smashed into halves

8 flat-leaf parsley stalks, roughly chopped

6 sprigs thyme

1 bay leaf, torn into 4 pieces

2 strips scrubbed lemon zest, halved

100–150ml dry alcoholic cider

1kg small–medium kipfler potatoes, scrubbed,
peeled and sliced in 2cm rounds

freshly ground white pepper

2 eschalots, finely chopped

1 cup chopped curly-leaf parsley

Vinaigrette

1 clove garlic, any green shoot removed, finely chopped

100ml extra virgin olive oil

20–30ml cider, seaweed, eschalot and fleur de sel vinegar*

sea salt and freshly ground white pepper

2 teaspoons Calvados [optional]

Serves 6

A Breton Mussel Salad

The tiny mussels from Breton have a wonderful sweet but salty character. The uncomplicated cooking of this region allows the flavour of these molluscs to shine, as this salad demonstrates. Look for smaller mussels from Spring Bay in Tasmania, which are excellent. They come cleaned in a neat package so all that remains to do is remove the odd tufts of the 'beards' protruding from their shells. The cider, seaweed, eschalot and fleur de sel vinegar is an essential ingredient in this salad.

1   Select a wide, deep frying pan that has a tight-fitting lid. Cook the mussels in 4 batches [overloading the pan will mean that some mussels will be overcooked]. Put a layer of mussels and one-quarter of the garlic, parsley, thyme, bay leaf and lemon zest into the pan, then add a splash of the cider. Cover the pan and place over the highest heat possible, then shake it from time to time while holding the lid on tightly; look for a whisper of steam emanating from the side of the lid. Lift off the lid and transfer the mussels to a large bowl using tongs the second they open. Strain the liquid through a sieve lined with moistened muslin cloth or paper towel and set aside. Repeat this process with the remaining mussels, garlic, parsley, thyme, bay leaf, lemon zest and cider until all the mussels have opened; discard any mussels that refuse to open.

2   Steam the potato for 10 minutes or until just tender; don't overcook. Immediately transfer the potato to a serving platter that will hold it in a thick layer. Drizzle with 60ml of the mussel cooking liquor, then season generously with pepper [salt is not needed as the mussel liquor is sufficiently salty] and scatter with the eschalots. When the potato has cooled, scatter with half the parsley and gently fold the ingredients together.

3   To make the vinaigrette, whisk together the ingredients, keeping in mind the saltiness of the mussel liquor, then drizzle about half over the potato.

4   Shell all but 24 of the mussels, examining each one for any bits of beard that must be discarded. Moisten the mussels with a little of the remaining vinaigrette, then toss lightly and scatter them over the potato, finishing with the parsley. Arrange the mussels in their shells attractively around the salad, then serve.

18–20 Love Bite, small truss or large cherry tomatoes*

125ml extra virgin olive oil, plus extra for rubbing and drizzling

sea salt and freshly ground black pepper

6–8 eggs [1 per serve], at fridge temperature

¼ cup small salted capers, soaked in warm water, rinsed and dried well with paper towel

100ml vegetable oil

2 × 1kg ribs dry-aged beef

4–6 pale inner stalks celery, cut into matchsticks, leaves roughly chopped, washed

1 bunch radishes, trimmed and washed, cut into small wedges

½ iceberg lettuce, washed and spin-dried, finely shredded

6–8 pale inner cos lettuce leaves

1 small head radicchio Treviso, washed and spin-dried, finely shredded

1 handful small watercress sprigs [about ½ bunch], washed and spin-dried

aged red-wine vinegar [such as Forum Cabernet vinegar*], to taste

4 dill-pickled cucumbers, cut into small pieces

1 bunch spring onions, white part only, trimmed

Horseradish mayonnaise

3 egg yolks

½ teaspoon hot English mustard

sea salt and freshly ground white or black pepper

120ml extra virgin olive oil

100ml grapeseed oil

20–25ml aged red-wine vinegar [such as Forum Cabernet vinegar*], to taste

2 tablespoons freshly grated horseradish* or prepared horseradish* [such as Tracklements brand; some prepared brands are very wet and should be drained]

Serves 6–8

Barbecued Rib of Beef Salad

My good friend Peter Wynne has a brilliant touch with beef, which he cooks in his giant Weber barbecue. I often bring Peter a rib of dry-aged 'Stockyard' or Wagyu beef from the wonderful new retail outlet Victor Churchill,* established by Vic's Premium Quality Meats in Woollahra's Queen Street shopping village. Those familiar with the locale will know the shop by its former name Churchill's. It has been a butcher's shop since the doors first opened in 1876.

Ideally, the beef should be generously seasoned and rubbed with olive oil ten hours before cooking, then placed uncovered in the fridge and removed one hour prior to cooking. Peter suggests cooking the beef in a Weber for thirty minutes, then leaving it to rest for thirty minutes before carving.

1 Preheat the oven to 120°C. Slice a tiny piece from the base of the tomatoes so that they will sit upright. Run a paring knife around the middle of each tomato to stop them from bursting as they cook. Select a wide ovenproof frying pan big enough to hold the tomatoes in one layer without touching. Pour 125ml olive oil into a small bowl and roll each tomato through the oil, then season with salt and pepper. Sit them upright in the pan, cover and roast for 15–20 minutes. Remove from the oven.

2 Prick the eggs with a fine pin then boil for 9 minutes. Refresh under cold running water. Shell and halve them.

3 Fry the capers in hot vegetable oil for 20 seconds, then dry on paper towel.

4 To make the horseradish mayonnaise, whisk the egg yolks, mustard, salt and a generous amount of pepper in a mixing bowl. Slowly add the combined oils in a fine stream, whisking continuously and taking care not to add more oil before the previous addition is absorbed. Continue adding the remaining oil until quite thick, then acidulate with a little vinegar, whisk in the horseradish and season to taste. The texture should be thick enough to coat the salad ingredients and should taste really hot and a bit acidic. Cover closely with plastic film and leave at room temperature until required.

5 Heat a covered barbecue until hot, then cook the beef with the lid on for 30 minutes. Remove and cover lightly with foil, then leave to rest for 30 minutes.

6 Moisten the celery, radish, iceberg, cos, radicchio, watercress, tomatoes and egg with a generous thread of oil and a splash of vinegar, then gently toss with your hands. Distribute half the salad leaves evenly between 6–8 plates. Finish with the remaining salad. Distribute the cucumber and spring onion. Dress with mayonnaise.

7 Remove all the fat from the beef and examine a rib; you'll notice several muscles. I separate these and discard any fatty connective tissue before carving. Carve thinly and fold the longer slices over, then distribute between the plates. Sprinkle salt on the beef and serve.

1 small clove garlic, any green shoot removed, smashed, and 2 cloves garlic, smashed	1 × 1.8kg free-range chicken [preferably Barossa or Glenloth]
½ teaspoon sea salt	24 thin spears asparagus [about 4 bunches]
20ml pistachio nut oil	3 litres water
extra virgin olive oil, for cooking	juice of ½ lemon
1 cup flat-leaf parsley [about ½ bunch], washed and spin-dried, leaves picked and lightly chopped, stalks roughly chopped	3 firm ripe peaches [preferably a white slipstone variety]
	ice cubes
¼ cup lightly chopped French tarragon leaves, stalks reserved	3 baby cos lettuces, coarse outer leaves discarded, each cut in 3 lengthwise
½ cup lightly chopped chervil	1 handful small watercress sprigs, washed and spin-dried
freshly ground white pepper	crusty baguettes, to serve

Chicken Salad with Asparagus, Peaches & Pistachio Nut Vinaigrette

This is a main course for a special summer lunch. It may be assembled some time ahead of serving; however, the chicken should be dressed while still warm so that it absorbs the flavours of the pistachio nut vinaigrette. It is interesting to see how dishes evolve over time and this is a case in point. When I wrote this recipe for a cooking class in 2001, it relied on tomatoes and celery for the salad ingredients. The asparagus appeared a few years later, and now the sweetness of peaches seems just right. Pistachio oil is a brilliant ingredient made by Le Blanc in France; only use it in combination with a vegetable oil and refrigerate the remainder since it is quite volatile.

Season the chicken with the herb-scented oil the night before your lunch and leave it uncovered in the fridge so that the skin dries out – this will produce a lovely golden crust. Sit the bird on a small cake-cooling rack or trivet placed over a plate.

1   Work the small clove of garlic and salt to a paste with the flat side of a knife, then mix this with the pistachio oil and 20–40ml olive oil. Combine the parsley leaves, tarragon and chervil with the garlic oil, then season with pepper. Taste for saltiness; it should be slightly salty.

2   Using your fingers and starting at the neck end of the chicken, gently ease the skin away from the breast, taking care not to pierce the skin. Do the same with the thigh but leave the leg joint untouched since the skin can break easily.

3   Use a piping bag without a nozzle or your fingers to work in the prepared oil mixture under the skin to cover the flesh. This is a messy job so do it on a shallow tray so as not to lose any seasoning. Put the remaining 2 cloves garlic and the roughly chopped parsley stalks into the cavity. Don't be concerned if some of the oil finishes up on the outside of the skin. Refrigerate the chicken uncovered to allow the skin to dry.

4   Take the chicken out of the fridge at least 30 minutes before cooking. Preheat the oven to 180°C. Rub the chicken all over with olive oil, salt and pepper, rubbing gently until the skin feels sweaty. Place the bird on an oiled cake-cooling rack in a roasting pan and roast on one side for 15 minutes; turn over and roast for another 15 minutes. Reduce the temperature to 160°C, then turn the bird breast-side up, baste with the pan juices and roast for a further 25–30 minutes until golden brown.

5   Crumple lots of foil into a deep bowl. Using a roasting fork inserted into the neck-end of the chicken as well as your hand, transfer the bird breast-side down into the bowl; it should sit evenly. Cover lightly with foil and rest for 30 minutes before carving.

6   Meanwhile, break the coarse ends off the asparagus; it will break at the point where it is tender. Trim the ends to neaten them. Blanch the asparagus in a saucepan of boiling salted water for 2 minutes or so, keeping it slightly undercooked. Refresh under cold running water, then drain well.

Pistachio nut vinaigrette

120ml pistachio oil	
40ml grapeseed oil	
40ml verjuice*	
¼ cup snipped French tarragon	
½ cup finely chopped chives	

1 pale inner stalk celery, washed and very finely diced

sea salt and freshly ground white pepper

2 teaspoons lime juice

60g pistachio nut kernels, blanched, skinned and roughly chopped

Serves 6

7 Bring 2 saucepans, each containing 1.5 litres of water, to the boil and have a bowl of iced water at the ready. Add the lemon juice to one pan. Plunge the peaches, one at time, into the pan of plain water for 30 seconds or so until the skin looks slightly wrinkled, then transfer immediately to a bowl of iced water; the skins should slip off easily. Return to the iced water.

8 Cut each peach into 8 segments and lower these into the boiling lemony water for 10 seconds. Transfer immediately to the iced water to stop them cooking. Drain and pat dry with paper towel [cover with plastic film if this step is done ahead of time].

9 To make the vinaigrette, combine the pistachio oil, grapeseed oil, verjuice, tarragon, chives and celery. Season with salt and pepper and adjust the acidity with lime juice. Toast the pistachio nuts in the oven at 150°C for 5–10 minutes, keeping an eye on them since they burn easily. Add immediately to the vinaigrette while they are hot.

10 Carve the chicken by first removing the leg and thigh joints. Remove the drumsticks, then run the knife along the thigh bones to cut the thighs in 2; dislodge and discard the bones. Run the knife as close as possible to the central breastbone, cutting through the wing joint and easing away the breast, which can be carefully pulled away from the carcass in one piece. Carve each breast on the diagonal into 4–5 slices. Moisten the warm chicken with some of the vinaigrette and leave for 10 minutes for the flavours to mingle.

11 Distribute the cos lettuce on a platter. Arrange the chicken on and around the lettuce, then drizzle with most of the vinaigrette. Place the asparagus in bundles of 3 here and there, along with the peaches and watercress, then moisten the watercress with the remaining vinaigrette. Serve this splendid salad immediately while it looks so fresh. Crusty baguettes should be the only accompaniment.

1 clove garlic, smashed	**Chicken liver croûtons**
extra virgin olive oil, for cooking	extra virgin olive oil, for cooking
2 tablespoons rosemary leaves, roughly chopped	sea salt and freshly ground white pepper
3 tablespoons thyme leaves	6 chicken livers, fat and any greenish marks trimmed off
6 spatchcocks,* butterfly style [as prepared by the butcher]	6 × 4cm × 1cm rounds sourdough bread
freshly ground white pepper	¼ cup finely chopped curly-leaf parsley
100g Puy-style lentils	**Vinaigrette**
½ small carrot, finely diced [to yield 2 tablespoons]	60ml extra virgin olive oil
sea salt	40ml grapeseed oil
12 small eschalots	sea salt and freshly ground white pepper
1 handful each rocket and watercress sprigs, washed and spin-dried	20ml lemon juice, or to taste
3 leaves radicchio, washed and spin-dried, torn	**Serves 6**
1 head witlof, damaged outer leaves removed, thinly sliced lengthwise	

Salad of Grilled Spatchcock with Lentils, Roasted Eschalots & Chicken Liver Croûtons

A perfectly grilled spatchcock is deliciously sweet and moist. Matched with the nuttiness of lentils, savoury and bitter leaves and a burst of flavour from the chicken livers, it makes a really satisfying main course.

1 Rub 2 roasting pans or large baking trays with the garlic and moisten generously with olive oil, then scatter over half the rosemary and thyme. Season the spatchcocks on both sides lightly with pepper and lay them, skin-side down, on the herbs. Scatter with the remaining rosemary and thyme, moisten with more olive oil and leave to marinate for 1 hour.

2 Preheat the oven to 160°C. Put the lentils, carrot, 20ml olive oil and ¼ teaspoon salt into a small saucepan. Bring to the boil and simmer over low heat for 20 minutes or until tender but not soft.

3 Meanwhile, moisten the eschalots with a little olive oil and bake in a small ovenproof frying pan for 25–30 minutes or until they test almost tender when pierced with a fine skewer. Transfer to a plate to cool, then peel carefully. Set aside.

4 Make the vinaigrette by mixing the extra virgin and grapeseed oils, salt and pepper, finishing with enough lemon juice to achieve a fresh acidity.

5 Preheat a large cast-iron chargrill, overhead griller or 2 large frying pans. Moisten with olive oil and, when quite hot, cook the lightly salted spatchcocks, skin-side down, for 3–4 minutes, taking care they don't burn. Turn over and cook for another few minutes or until cooked. Pierce the thigh joint with a fine skewer; the juices should be pale pink. Transfer to a warm tray to rest, lightly covered with foil.

6 To start preparing the chicken liver croûtons, heat 2 teaspoons olive oil in a small frying pan over high heat until very hot but not smoking. Season the livers and sear quickly until coloured on both sides; they should remain pink inside. Transfer to the plate with the eschalots. Reduce the oven to 150°C. Brush the bread with olive oil and bake for 5 minutes to gain a little colour. Use a fork to lightly crush a chicken liver onto each croûton. Finish with a good sprinkling of parsley, then cover loosely with foil. Turn off the oven, then put in the croûtons and 6 main course plates, leaving the door ajar.

7 Halve the eschalots, then distribute with the lentils around each croûton and moisten with a little vinaigrette.

8 Carve the drumsticks away from the breasts and place on either side of the croûtons. Turn the spatchcocks over and pull away the ribcage along with any remaining little bones. Carve on the diagonal from the wing to the tip of the breast, then transfer to a mixing bowl. Moisten with the remaining vinaigrette and toss gently.

9 Distribute the leaves around the drumsticks, then add the breast slices. Drizzle with the vinaigrette remaining in the bowl and serve immediately.

1 × 1.8kg free-range chicken [preferably Barossa or Glenloth]	boiling water, as required
sea salt and freshly ground white pepper	150g baby carrots, scrubbed and the tops discarded
1 small head garlic, halved crosswise	½ teaspoon caster sugar
¼ cup French tarragon [about 1 bunch], roughly chopped	2 eggs, at fridge temperature
50g unsalted butter	150g celeriac, cut into 5mm matchsticks
2 litres light chicken stock [homemade or good-quality vacuum-packed]	2 handfuls small watercress sprigs, washed and spin-dried
	crusty baguettes, to serve

Chicken & Tarragon Mayonnaise Salad

This salad is based on the traditional roast tarragon chicken from French bourgeois cuisine, which is arguably my favourite dish. I have added carrots and celeriac for contrast in flavour and texture, as well as watercress for a touch of spiciness. The chicken may be cooked well in advance and cooled in the poaching liquor. To make stunning chicken sandwiches on white bread, delete the carrot and replace the celeriac with finely diced celery; they will be a hit.

1 Take the chicken out of the fridge at least 30 minutes before cooking. Remove any fat deposits from the cavity of the chicken and rinse under cold running water. Dry inside using paper towel, then season well and insert the garlic, tarragon and butter. Cut a small slit between the leg and breast on both sides, taking care not to damage the breast flesh.

2 Select a stockpot with a tight-fitting lid that will hold the chicken comfortably without too much space to spare; check by putting the bird in the pan before adding the stock. Remove the chicken, pour the stock into the pan, then bring to a rapid boil [have a large kettle of boiling water ready in case more liquid is needed; the exact quantity required will depend on the size of the pot]. Lower the chicken into the stock, then top up with boiling water to cover well. Return to a rapid boil, then cover with the lid. Turn off the heat and leave untouched for 1 hour; remove the pot from the element if cooking with electricity or induction.

3 When the chicken is ready, remove the lid and carefully turn the chicken so it is breast-side down, then leave to rest in the stock for 20 minutes.

4 Meanwhile, to make the tarragon mayonnaise, whisk the egg yolks, mustard, salt and a generous amount of pepper in a mixing bowl. Slowly add the combined oils in a fine stream, whisking continuously and taking care not to add more oil before the previous addition is absorbed. Continue adding the remaining oil until quite thick, then acidulate with a little vinegar and season to taste. Stir in the tarragon. The texture should be quite thick. Taste and adjust the seasoning.

5 Slice the thin ends of the carrots into 5mm-thick rounds, then split the thicker tops in half lengthwise and slice to the same thickness. Transfer to a saucepan of cold salted water with the sugar, then bring to the boil over high heat and boil for 2–3 minutes until firm but tender. Drain and dry well with a clean tea towel, then set aside.

6 Prick the eggs with a fine pin, then cook in a saucepan of boiling water for 10 minutes. Remove, cool under cold running water, then shell and roughly chop into 1cm pieces.

7 Combine the carrot, celeriac and egg in a bowl and moisten with a few spoonfuls of the mayonnaise, then fold gently with a wooden or plastic spoon so as not to damage them. Cover and refrigerate until the chicken is ready.

Tarragon mayonnaise

3 egg yolks

2 teaspoons Dijon mustard [preferably the tarragon variety]

½ teaspoon sea salt, to start

freshly ground white pepper

120ml grapeseed oil

100ml extra virgin olive oil, or more as needed

aged white-wine vinegar [such as Forum Chardonnay vinegar*], to taste

¼ cup lightly chopped French tarragon

Serves 6

8 Drain the chicken and place on a platter, reserving the stock. Carefully remove the skin with your fingertips and discard it. Dislodge the drumsticks and breast meat by running a knife down either side of the breast bone, then cut the wing-joint free; you will be able to pull away the breasts with a gentle tug. Check the carcass for any remaining flesh and remove. Cut the leg from the thigh and cut the flesh into smallish dice. Tear the breasts into threads, following the natural grain of the meat.

9 To prepare the stock for storing, skim off any fat on the surface with a ladle, then use paper towel to eradicate all traces of fat. Bring to the boil over high heat and reduce by half. Cool to room temperature, then refrigerate. Transfer to small containers, label, date and freeze for use in a risotto or soup.

10 Transfer the chicken flesh to a large bowl, then moisten with just enough mayonnaise to coat the flesh lightly. Fold in the carrot, celeriac and egg mixture using your hands. Taste and correct the seasoning; spike with a touch more vinegar if it needs a lift. Transfer to a platter and surround with the watercress, then serve with crusty baguettes.

Carrot, Potato and Chicken Salad – a supper dish for two

Here is a simple and attractive salad to make use of leftover roast chicken breast. Dice equal quantities of peeled waxy potatoes and peeled carrots and cook them separately in salted boiling water. Drain and combine with skinned and diced chicken and 1 tablespoon sliced cornichons* to provide some acidity. Mix 20ml hazelnut oil with 40ml vegetable oil in a bowl rubbed with a smashed clove of garlic. Discard the garlic debris. Moisten the salad with the vinaigrette and toss. Serve garnished with chopped skinned hazelnuts that have been toasted in a 160°C oven until pale golden. Substitute 3mm matchsticks of leg ham if you don't have any leftover chicken.

1 × 1.8kg free-range chicken [preferably Barossa or Glenloth], loose fat removed from the carcass

½ teaspoon saffron stamens

¼ teaspoon ground turmeric

4 cloves garlic, any green shoot removed

sea salt

1 head fennel, outer ribs removed, base trimmed, cut lengthwise into 1cm-thick slices

2 wide strips scrubbed lemon zest

2 wide strips scrubbed orange zest

60ml verjuice⁕

100ml light chicken stock

40ml extra virgin olive oil

freshly ground white pepper

200g basmati rice

2cm piece cinnamon stick

2–3 firm ripe tomatoes⁕ [such as Love Bites or Romas]

200g small seedless grapes

80g chopped blanched almonds

Vinaigrette

50ml reduced chicken cooking liquor

100ml extra virgin olive oil

2 pieces preserved lemon, flesh discarded, skin finely diced

aged sherry vinegar, to taste

salt and freshly ground white pepper

Serves 6

Salad of Saffron-scented Chicken with Rice, Fennel & Grapes

Here a Barossa chicken is cooked in a broth enriched with saffron and fennel, which contribute a superb colour and unique flavour to complement the delicacy of the basmati rice. Small seedless grapes add a sweet and sour freshness to this salad, which is dressed with a vinaigrette enriched with chicken jus and tomatoes. Serve during the cooler months followed by A Dried & Citrus Fruit Salad on page 208. You will need to use only some of the chicken cooking liquor. The remainder may be used to flavour a soup or some couscous; add diced preserved lemon and lots of roughly chopped flat-leaf parsley to the latter to serve alongside grilled fish.

1   Joint the chicken by removing the full legs and separating the thighs from the drumsticks. Use a sharp knife or poultry shears to cut just below the base of the breasts down to the wing joints, then detach the backbone section. Use a sharp knife to split the breasts on either side of the breastbone. The rib cage will still be attached, which helps to keep the breast moist while it cooks. It can be pulled away easily after the chicken is cooked.

2   Preheat the oven to 100°C. Put the saffron and turmeric on a saucer in the oven for 5 minutes.

3   Chop and crush 2 of the garlic cloves with 1 teaspoon salt to a paste on a chopping board using the blade of a knife, then transfer to a wide-based frying pan or casserole with a tight-fitting lid that will accommodate the chicken in one layer. Add the saffron and turmeric, fennel, zests, verjuice and chicken stock, then bring to the boil over high heat. Add the olive oil, ½ teaspoon salt and some pepper. Reduce the heat to low and add

the jointed chicken to the pan. Add as little water as possible to come halfway up the chicken, then place a piece of baking paper on the surface. Cover with the lid and cook very gently over the lowest heat possible for 25 minutes, then turn the chicken over, replace the baking paper and lid and cook for another 15 minutes or until the chicken is very tender.

4   Meanwhile, cook the rice with the cinnamon as directed on the packet. Tip the rice into a large mixing bowl and use 2 forks to fluff up the grains, discarding the cinnamon.

5   Peel the tomatoes using a vegetable peeler, then cut into 4 wedges each, remove the seeds and cut each segment into 3 pieces. Wash the grapes and cut each in half lengthwise or quarters if large. Toast the almonds over low heat in a dry frying pan, then transfer to a plate.

6   Transfer the chicken to a platter and reserve the cooking liquor. When the chicken is cool enough to handle, cut into neat little dice, discarding the bones. Chop the fennel similarly, then add both to the rice; do not combine just yet.

7   To make the vinaigrette, degrease 150ml of the chicken cooking liquor with paper towel, then reduce over high heat by two-thirds [to about 50ml]. Pour into a bowl and whisk until somewhat cool, then whisk in the vinaigrette ingredients. Taste and adjust the seasoning; it should be slightly salty. Pour the vinaigrette over the chicken, fennel and rice, then add the tomato, grapes and almonds. Fold gently with your hands, then transfer to a platter or deep salad bowl. Best served at room temperature.

4–5 duck breasts [preferably Chinese Pekin or Aylesbury], skin scored on the diagonal [don't penetrate the flesh]

40ml soy sauce

30ml sesame oil

20ml rice vinegar or white-wine vinegar

1 tablespoon white sugar

3 red peppers, washed, seeded and cut into fine julienne

50g Japanese pickled ginger [amazu shoga], each slice cut in half

grapeseed oil or vegetable oil spray, for cooking

sea salt

2–3 handfuls small watercress sprigs, washed and spin-dried

24 lychees, peeled

½ large firm ripe mango, cut into long 3mm-wide matchsticks

6 large snow peas [mange-tout], threads removed, cut into fine julienne

Serves 6

Duck Salad Chinoise

I was lucky to be the executive chef of Pavilion on the Park in the Domain in the late 1970s. I guess the restaurant's style would be considered 'international' in today's terminology since we drew our repertoire from French, Italian and Thai culinary traditions. The essential difference about Pavilion's cooking was its reliance on offering the best of the day's market – *cuisine du marché* as it is known in France.

Our fruit and vegetable supplier, Andrew, would call me at about 6.30am with a list of the best the market had to offer, then I would plan the day's à la carte lunch and table d'hôte dinner menus. Such fun, and the team's adrenalin would pump as the morning's *mise en place* [preparation] was done. We were so busy as to turn over virtually all the produce within the two services; now that's really fresh cooking!

This pretty little salad is an example of my Pavilion business partner Mogens Bay Esbensen's spontaneous creativity. Mogens had spent most of his working life in Thailand and had a broad experience of Asian cuisine, apart from being 'born to cook'.

1 Take the duck breasts out of the fridge 15 minutes before grilling them.

2 Meanwhile, using a large bowl, mix the soy, sesame oil, vinegar and sugar to make the marinade, then add the peppers and ginger.

3 Heat a cast-iron chargrill or heavy-based frying pan that will accommodate the duck breasts comfortably over high heat. Have 2 large dinner plates on hand or a baking tray and chopping board large enough to hold all the breasts on the tray [the second plate or chopping board is placed on top of the duck while it rests].

4 Moisten the very hot grill or pan lightly with oil. Rub a little salt into the duck skin to penetrate the cut surfaces, then cook the breasts, skin-side down, checking the colouring after 1 minute or less and if they are browning too quickly reduce temperature to medium. After about 2 minutes the skins should have coloured nicely so flip the breasts over and cook for another minute or so. To test whether the duck is ready press a finger against a breast; it should feel springy.

5 Transfer the duck to a plate or baking tray, skin-side up, then put the other plate or chopping board on top and leave the duck to rest for 5 minutes.

6 Carve the breasts crosswise into thin slices with a very sharp knife, then fold into the marinade.

7 Scatter 6 flat entrée plates with watercress, then distribute the duck, peppers, ginger, lychees and mango equally. Moisten with the marinade, scatter with the snow peas, toss lightly, then serve immediately.

8 brown pickling onions

extra virgin olive oil

1.2kg baby squid

sea salt and freshly ground white pepper

½ × 450g can chick peas, drained, skins pinched off

2 handfuls small Vietnamese mint sprigs, washed and spin-dried

1 handful Thai basil leaves

½ cup chives, cut into 2cm lengths

3 radicchio leaves, washed and spin-dried, torn into small pieces

2 handfuls dandelion leaves, washed and spin-dried, torn into small pieces, or 2 handfuls watercress sprigs

40ml grapeseed oil

2 cloves garlic, any green shoot removed, roughly chopped

1 fresh birds eye chilli, seeded and finely chopped

Hot smoked paprika vinaigrette

1 small clove garlic, smashed

½ teaspoon hot smoked paprika* [such as Spanish La Chinata brand]

80ml extra virgin olive oil

2 teaspoons aged sherry vinegar

2 teaspoons lime juice, or to taste

sea salt and freshly ground white pepper

Serves 6

Baby Squid Salad with Chick Peas, Fresh Herbs & Hot Smoked Paprika Vinaigrette

This rustic salad is ideal for a casual lunch. Roasted pickling onions and chick peas provide the foundation flavours to contrast the sweetness of the seared squid. Mint, chives and dandelion offer a lively spike to match the spiciness of the vinaigrette. Everything can be prepared ahead, leaving only the last-minute cooking of the squid, so there will be plenty of time to be with your guests, especially if you offer cheese and fruit to follow. The squid must be cooked in two batches over really high heat so that it remains moist.

1   Preheat the oven to 180°C. Discard any damaged skin from the onions and pierce them through their centres with a fine skewer, then roll in olive oil and wrap in foil. Bake for 30 minutes or until they are very tender when pierced with the fine skewer. Cool briefly, then unwrap and remove the skins. Cut each onion in half.

2   Meanwhile, clean each squid by twisting the head and pulling it away from the body; retain the tentacles but discard the head. Remove the flat, quill-like 'bone' from inside the body and discard. Rinse the body and pull off the outer brownish skin. Cut the body into 1cm-thick rings and cut the tentacles in half. Drain the squid in a colander, then pat dry and season with salt and pepper.

3   To make the vinaigrette, rub a small mixing bowl with the garlic and discard the debris. Toast the paprika in a dry frying pan over low heat for 20 seconds or until aromatic. Whisk together the remaining ingredients, then whisk in the paprika directly from the pan. Taste and adjust the seasoning.

4   Place the onion, chick peas, herbs, radicchio and dandelion or watercress in a large mixing bowl and cover with plastic film.

5   When ready to serve, heat half the grapeseed oil in a wok to smoking point over the highest heat possible, then stir-fry half the seasoned squid for 30–60 seconds, adding half the garlic and chilli in the last 10 seconds – for best results use the highest heat possible. Turn into a large bowl with any juices, then wipe out the wok with paper towel. Repeat with the remaining oil, squid, garlic and chilli. Leave to cool for a few minutes, then toss with the vinaigrette.

6   Add the squid mixture to the bowl of leaves and herbs, then toss gently with your hands. Serve on a deep platter.

10–15 quite firm Love Bite tomatoes* or 8 vine-ripened or truss tomatoes

120ml extra virgin olive oil, plus extra if needed

sea salt and freshly ground black pepper

600–700g orecchiette pasta

4 kipfler potatoes, cut into 5mm dice

½ cup roughly chopped flat-leaf parsley

¼ cup tiny salted capers, soaked in warm water, rinsed and dried with paper towel

25g Parmigiano Reggiano, very finely grated

Serves 6

Orecchiette with Roasted Tomatoes & Potatoes Tossed in Tomato Juices

This room-temperature pasta salad came about when the cupboard was almost bare apart from these ingredients. *Orecchiette* literally means 'little ears' in Italian and they are hand-shaped accordingly. Their ovate form allows them to capture a wet sauce, as long as some finely grated parmesan is added to assist this process when the dish is tossed. I had some Love Bite tomatoes* from Sydney provedore Fratelli Fresh on hand and decided to roast them slowly with some fine extra virgin olive oil so as to create a tomato roasting liquor that could be tossed with diced kipfler potatoes. Finishing with some roughly chopped flat-leaf parsley and capers made this a delicious impromptu salad.

1 Preheat the oven to 150°C. Slice a tiny piece from the base of the tomatoes so that they will sit upright while roasting. Run a paring knife around the middle of each tomato to stop them from bursting as they cook. Select a shallow ovenproof frying pan that has a lid, large enough to hold the tomatoes in one layer without touching [or use 2 smaller pans]. Pour the olive oil into a small bowl and roll each tomato through the oil, seasoning with salt and pepper. Sit them upright in the pan, put on the lid and bake for 20 minutes or more, depending on their size. They should test very soft when pierced with a fine skewer and the skin will have retracted. There should also be a lot of delicious tomato oil in the pan. Remove from the oven.

2 Warm a heatproof salad bowl in the oven for a few minutes. While the tomatoes are roasting, cook the pasta in a saucepan of boiling salted water following packet instructions until quite al dente.

3 Steam or boil the potatoes for 8 minutes or so, keeping them on the slightly firm side. Transfer the potatoes to the warm bowl, then add the tomato oil and toss gently. Drain the pasta well and combine with the potatoes and tomatoes, breaking up the tomatoes with a fork. Add the parsley, capers and parmesan, and a little more oil if the salad looks a bit dry. Adjust the seasoning, then fold together with your hands.

4 Allow to cool to room temperature and serve.

6 × 160g [3cm-thick] slices tuna

1 × 250–300g bulb celeriac

1–2 heads baby fennel, outer ribs and stalks removed [retain some of the fronds if still attached]

6 ripe Love Bite or Roma tomatoes,* each cut into 6 wedges

10 basil leaves, torn into small pieces

80ml extra virgin olive oil

1 teaspoon cider vinegar*

sea salt and freshly ground white pepper

Fried basil leaves

120–150ml grapeseed oil

20 basil leaves

Court-bouillon

2 litres cold water

250ml dry white wine

40ml tarragon vinegar

1 small onion, sliced

½ stalk celery, thinly sliced

½ small carrot, sliced

bouquet garni* [a few sprigs thyme, 6 parsley stalks, 1 bay leaf and 2 strips lemon zest all wrapped in a muslin cloth and tied with kitchen twine]

3 teaspoons sea salt

6 cracked black peppercorns

Aïoli

1 large or 2 small cloves garlic, any green shoot removed

½ teaspoon sea salt and some freshly ground white pepper

2 egg yolks

2 teaspoons Dijon mustard

100ml extra virgin olive oil

100–120ml grapeseed oil

2 teaspoons lemon juice, or to taste

2 teaspoons yoghurt

Serves 6

Tuna, Tomato, Celeriac & Fennel Salad with Aïoli

Here, the tuna is poached off the heat quite briefly so that it remains undercooked. This technique produces a very moist texture and the flavour is enriched by the aïoli and the fried basil leaves. Crunchy texture comes from the celeriac, fennel and firm ripe tomatoes, preferably the Love Bite cultivar. Begin the meal with homemade poultry terrine or Maggie Beer's delicious Pheasant Paté, olives, cornichons* and sourdough toast and finish with a couple of quality bought ices; an excellent little menu and not too much work for the cook. If you prefer, the first three steps may be done several hours ahead.

1 Bring the court-bouillon ingredients slowly to the boil over low heat, skim the surface, then simmer for 20–30 minutes. Strain into a deep frying pan with a tight-fitting lid that will hold the tuna in one layer. Adjust the seasoning to slightly salty and set aside.

2 Remove the tuna from the fridge 30 minutes before cooking.

3 To make the aïoli, crush the garlic with the salt on a chopping board and work into a smooth paste with the flat side of a knife. Transfer to a small bowl, then add the pepper, yolks and mustard. Whisk well, then slowly add the combined oils in a fine stream, whisking continuously and taking care not to add more oil before the previous addition is absorbed. Continue adding the remaining oil until quite thick, then season to taste. The texture should be rather thick. Add 2 teaspoons lemon juice to freshen the taste, then whisk in the yoghurt. If the sauce is still thick, add a little more lemon juice or water.

4 Up to 45 minutes before serving the salad, return the court-bouillon to a rolling boil over high heat, then lower the tuna into the pan. Allow to return to the boil, put on the lid and remove from the heat. Leave untouched for 8 minutes. Transfer the tuna from the court-bouillon to a plate and pat dry with paper towel.

5 Peel the celeriac and cut into 3mm-thick slices with a very sharp knife, then cut into matchsticks. Cut the fennel into quarters lengthwise, then shave very thinly with a mandoline.* Combine the celeriac, fennel, tomato and torn basil in a mixing bowl, then moisten with the olive oil and vinegar and season with salt and pepper. Toss gently.

6 Meanwhile, for the fried basil leaves, heat the grapeseed oil in a small saucepan over medium heat and fry the basil leaves for 20 seconds. Drain on paper towel immediately.

7 Place a piece of tuna on each of 6 main course plates and coat generously with the aïoli. Arrange the salad beside the tuna, then scatter with the fried basil leaves and serve with a bowl of aïoli to the side.

2 pale inner stalks celery, cut into 5mm dice

2 cloves garlic, any green shoot removed

sea salt

80–100ml extra virgin olive oil

a trace of cayenne pepper

9 × 3mm-thick slices ciabatta bread

18 baby cos lettuce leaves, washed and spin-dried

5–6 dill-pickled cucumbers, cut into quarters lengthwise

18 × 2mm-thick slices rolled leg ham [preferably Kurobuta]

2 handfuls mixed salad leaves [including tiny sprigs watercress and rocket, 3–4cm witlof tips, baby spinach leaves and thinly shaved radicchio leaves], washed and spin-dried [except the witlof]

1 large firm ripe avocado,* peeled, seeded and quartered

250g teardrop or cherry tomatoes, halved

2 spring onions, trimmed and sliced on the diagonal [including some of the green tops]

Mustard mayonnaise

2 egg yolks

1 tablespoon Dijon or English mustard

½ teaspoon sea salt

freshly ground black pepper

100ml grapeseed oil

100ml extra virgin olive oil

2–3 teaspoons aged white-wine vinegar [such as Forum Chardonnay vinegar*]

Serves 6

Leg Ham 'Sandwich' Salad

I really enjoy the texture and more delicious flavour of multiple layers of very thin slices of ham over the chunkier option of thickly sliced ham since the latter tends to have a duller taste. This is especially important when you are making a ham sandwich with good butter, mustard and perhaps some lettuce. Inspired to take the sandwich idea a little further, I've used the key elements to create a radical little salad for a bit of fun. It could be served as a substantial snack with a beer while watching the footy or a DVD.

The following recipe may look complicated but will be easy if everything is prepared ahead; it is then only a matter of assembling the salad when everyone feels hungry. You might like to use a good-quality ready-made mayonnaise and whisk in mustard to taste along with the celery. Similarly, spicy or herb-flavoured grissini could replace the ciabatta toasts to make things easier.

1 Preheat the oven to 150°C. Meanwhile, to make the mayonnaise, whisk the egg yolks, mustard, salt and a generous amount of pepper in a mixing bowl. Slowly add the combined oils in a fine stream, whisking continuously and taking care not to add more oil before the previous addition is absorbed. Continue adding the remaining oil until quite thick, then acidulate with a little vinegar and season to taste. The texture should be rather thick. Add the celery and season to taste. Dilute ¼ cup of the mayonnaise with very little water to make a thinner dressing that will just coat the leaves. Leftovers can be stored closely covered with plastic film in the fridge for up to a week.

2 Crush the garlic with the salt on a chopping board, working it into a smooth paste with the flat side of a knife. Transfer to a small bowl, then mix in the olive oil and cayenne. Paint the ciabatta slices on one side, then dry them in the oven for 10–15 minutes or until crisp and pale golden.

3 Lay out the cos leaves and top each one with a piece of cucumber and 1 tablespoon mayonnaise. Crumble 2 or 3 slices of the toast over the cos leaves.

4 Place the ham in 2 stacks on a chopping board and cut each into quarters to produce 72 pieces. Separate into 18 stacks of 4 slices.

5 Moisten the mixed leaves with a very little of the diluted mayonnaise and toss gently with your hands, then scatter over 6 deep entrée plates. Cut the avocado quarters into 5mm-thick slices and distribute between the serves. Add the tomato and spring onion. Tuck 3 filled cos leaves into each salad and lay the ham loosely over the top. Break the remaining ciabatta toasts roughly and scatter over the leaves.

	Braised lentils	
1 clove garlic, smashed	**Braised lentils**
50g [4 tablespoons] quatre-épices	200g Puy-style lentils
5 sprigs thyme, leaves picked	½ onion, peeled
6 skinless chicken breasts [800–900g]	½ carrot, roughly sliced
300–400ml olive oil	1 bay leaf
2 pale inner stalks celery, cut into 5mm-thick slices	½ teaspoon sea salt
3 pieces preserved lemon, flesh discarded, skin roughly chopped	600ml water
	Vinaigrette
1½ cups small Vietnamese mint leaves, washed and spin-dried	150ml extra virgin olive oil
1 cup torn coriander leaves, plunged in cold running water and shaken dry	40ml pistachio oil
	40ml verjuice*
1 handful flat-leaf parsley leaves, washed and spin-dried	1 tablespoon double cream
⅓ cup finely chopped garlic chives	lime juice, to taste
sea salt and freshly ground white pepper	sea salt and freshly ground white pepper
6 medium cos lettuce leaves, washed and spin-dried	**Serves 6**
60g pistachio nut kernels, blanched, chopped and toasted	

Spiced Chicken with a Lentil & Fresh Herb Salad

This recipe appeared in my first book, *French*. It is such a lovely salad that I thought I would revisit it and give it a new identity by adding lots of fresh herbs, crisp cos leaves and preserved lemon. Finely chopped toasted pistachios add a sweet nutty note. For the spicing, I have employed the classic quatre-épices mixture, which is used principally in charcuterie. This is a melange of seven parts allspice and one part each cinnamon, cloves and nutmeg. While it is easy to grind with a mortar and pestle or spice mill, Herbie's Spices* have their own excellent mixture.

You will need to begin making this salad at least three hours ahead of serving. Ideally, cook the chicken one hour ahead then avoid refrigeration if possible, since chilling will dull its flavour and take away its light texture.

1   Rub a wide shallow dish or container with the garlic then discard the debris. Combine the quatre-épices and thyme, then rub the mixture into the chicken. Cover and refrigerate for 1 hour, then turn the chicken, rub in the spice mixture again and leave for another hour. Remove from the fridge 30 minutes before cooking.

2   To make the braised lentils, inspect the lentils and discard any small stones, then rinse under cold running water. Put them into a large saucepan with the onion, carrot, bay leaf and salt. Add the water, bring to the boil, then simmer over low heat for 20 minutes; the lentils should be tender but offer a little bite. Leave to cool in the liquid, then remove the onion, carrot and bay leaf and drain.

3   Make the vinaigrette while the lentils are cooking by shaking the ingredients in a screw-top jar. It should be very well seasoned and taste slightly acidic. Moisten the lentils with some of the vinaigrette, then cover and set aside.

4   Select a wide-based frying pan or flameproof roasting pan that will accommodate the chicken in one layer. Add the oil and heat over medium heat until it registers 80°C on a candy thermometer.* Add the chicken; the temperature should drop to about 70°C. Cook the chicken at this temperature for 10–15 minutes or until the juices run slightly pink or clear. To test, transfer a breast to a plate then insert a fine skewer into the thickest part, holding a spoon under the incision to collect the juice.

5   Transfer the breasts to a plate to cool briefly, loosely covered with plastic film. Tear the chicken into threads, following the natural grain, then immediately moisten with vinaigrette for the best flavour.

6   Combine the chicken, celery, preserved lemon, herbs and lentils using your hands. Taste and adjust the seasoning. Place a spoonful of salad on each of 6 deep main course plates, put a cos leaf on top so that it projects above the plate. Distribute the remaining salad equally onto the leaves and scatter with pistachios. Drizzle the remaining vinaigrette around the salads, and serve.

Salads on the side

Salades d'accompagnement

30g soft brown sugar

sea salt

900g Queensland blue pumpkin, peeled, seeded and cut into 2cm dice

olive oil spray

1½ cups finely shredded radicchio

200g spinach leaves, washed and spin-dried, torn into small pieces

225g button mushrooms, stems removed, caps cut into quarters

Fried sage leaves

100ml vegetable oil or peanut oil

½ cup sage leaves

Spicy toasted almonds

¼ teaspoon cayenne pepper

¼ teaspoon fine salt

¼ teaspoon ground cumin

½ eggwhite, or a little more

120g blanched almonds, splintered or coarsely chopped

Dressing

60ml extra virgin olive oil

30ml almond oil or avocado oil

20ml verjuice*

2 teaspoons lime juice, or to taste

sea salt and freshly ground black pepper

Serves 6

Roast Pumpkin, Mushroom & Spinach Salad with Spicy Toasted Almonds

The sweetness of the pumpkin is contrasted by the acidity of the spinach and bitterness of the radicchio. Crisp fried sage leaves add an earthy touch and the spicy almonds provide a spark for the palate, while the mushrooms absorb all the flavours. The almonds can take up to two hours to roast and may be done well in advance of the other steps. Serve with ham off the bone, grilled lamb cutlets, or grilled or barbecued salmon or Hiramasa Ichiban kingfish. Also good with a roast chicken served at room temperature.

1   Preheat the oven to 110°C. To make the roasted almonds, sift the cayenne, salt and cumin into a mixing bowl, then whisk in just enough eggwhite to make a moist paste. Toss the almonds in the paste to barely coat them: if they look too wet spoon off the excess paste. Spread the almond mixture over a large baking sheet so that the nuts are separated. Bake for up to 2 hours, shaking the tray from time to time. Transfer to a tray lined with baking paper and leave to cool, then seal in an airtight container.

2   Sift the sugar and salt through a coarse sieve, then toss with the pumpkin. Spray lightly with olive oil, then toss and spray again for an even coating. Transfer to a baking tray and bake for 10 minutes. Turn the pumpkin with a spatula and continue to bake for another 10 minutes or until lightly caramelised. The pumpkin should still be a bit undercooked.

3   Place the pumpkin, radicchio, spinach and mushrooms in a large bowl and gently toss together.

4   For the fried sage leaves, heat the oil in a deep saucepan to 160°C and fry the sage leaves for 20 seconds or so until crisp. Drain immediately on paper towel.

5   To make the dressing, whisk the oils, verjuice and lime juice with a small pinch of salt and some pepper, then taste and correct the seasoning; it should taste quite acidic so add more lime juice if necessary.

6   Moisten the vegetables with about half the dressing and toss gently, then add more dressing and toss again. Transfer to a platter or individual plates and scatter with the toasted almonds and sage leaves, then serve.

1 × 450g can chick peas, drained, skins gently pinched off

3 Lebanese cucumbers, peeled and cut into 3mm dice

1 clove garlic, finely chopped

3 spring onions, bases trimmed, finely chopped [including a little of the green ends]

½ bunch mint or basil, torn into small pieces

3 pieces preserved lemon, flesh discarded, rind finely diced

sea salt and freshly ground black pepper

40–60ml extra virgin olive oil

a splash aged red-wine vinegar [such as Forum Cabernet vinegar*]

12 baby cos leaves [from about 2–3 lettuces], washed and spin-dried

Serves 6

Salad of Chick Peas, Cucumbers & Preserved Lemon

Sometimes a simple salad can lift a grilled fish or meat to an elegant little meal. This quickly prepared salad is also a good partner for a takeaway rotisserie chicken, such as one from Victor Churchill* in Woollahra, New South Wales.

1 Place the chick peas, cucumber, garlic, spring onions, mint or basil and preserved lemon in a bowl. Combine using your hands and taste for saltiness before seasoning with pepper. Moisten with the oil and vinegar.

2 Distribute between 12 cos leaves and serve 2 per person with your chosen fish or meat.

½ cup [50g] walnut kernels, broken

20ml walnut oil

2 large handfuls very small watercress sprigs, washed and spin-dried

¾ small celeriac, cut into thin matchsticks [about 1½ cups]

2 small pears [such as Josephine or Packham], on the firm side of ripe

a little lemon juice

Vinaigrette

40ml walnut oil

40ml vegetable oil

2–3 teaspoons cider vinegar*

sea salt and freshly ground white pepper

Serves 6

Watercress, Pear & Celeriac Salad

Here is a splendid salad to serve with mildly flavoured quail or confit rabbit legs accompanied by sautéed kipfler potatoes with garlic and parsley. Should there be some reduced chicken or game stock on hand add two teaspoons to the vinaigrette, in which case a touch more vinegar might be required.

1 Toss the walnut pieces and walnut oil thoroughly in a bowl, then toast in a frying pan over low heat until lightly coloured. Turn out onto a plate to cool.

2 To make the vinaigrette, whisk the oils and vinegar with some salt and pepper.

3 Place the watercress, celeriac and walnuts in a salad bowl, then add enough of the vinaigrette to moisten and toss.

4 Peel, quarter and remove the cores from the pears, then squeeze a little lemon juice over to stop them from discolouring. Shave the pear into 5mm-thick slices using a knife or mandoline* and scatter over the salad, tossing gently. Serve immediately.

½ cup [70g] pecan nut kernels, each broken into 2–3 pieces

vegetable oil spray

1½ bunches baby carrots, tops removed, peeled

sea salt

250g sugar snap peas, strings removed

200g celeriac or celery, cut into thin 4cm-long matchsticks

freshly ground white pepper

2 heads witlof, outer leaves removed, inner leaves separated

mustard cress [optional], to serve

Toasted coriander seed vinaigrette

3 teaspoons coriander seeds

40ml walnut oil

40ml extra virgin olive oil

60ml vegetable oil

sea salt and freshly ground black pepper

30ml cider vinegar*

Serves 6

Baby Carrot, Sugar Snap Pea & Celeriac Salad with Pecan Nuts & Toasted Coriander Seed Vinaigrette

Here is a full-textured, refreshing salad to accompany a mildly spiced fish curry or grilled pepper-crusted tuna steaks. For the latter, use a mixture of cracked white peppercorns with a good pinch of Sichuan pepper. Pat the tuna steaks with paper towel and spray very lightly with olive oil, then encrust with the pepper mixture, pressing it well into the fish on both sides. Place on a rack and refrigerate uncovered for 30–45 minutes to set the crust, then cook until rare in a heavy-based frying pan moistened with olive oil.

1 Preheat the oven to 150°C. Spread the pecans on a baking tray, spray lightly with vegetable oil and toast for 10 minutes or until golden.

2 Cut the carrots into 2cm lengths from their ends. Cut the thicker tops in half lengthwise and then into 2cm lengths so that they will cook evenly. Place in a saucepan and cover with cold salted water, then simmer for 4–5 minutes or until tender but still a little crisp. Drain and refresh under cold running water, then drain well. Pat dry with paper towel.

3 Plunge the sugar snaps into a saucepan of boiling salted water to blanch for 30 seconds once the water returns to the boil. Drain and refresh under cold running water, then drain well. Pat dry with paper towel.

4 To make the vinaigrette, toast the coriander seeds in a dry frying pan over low–medium heat for 1 minute or so or until aromatic, taking care to keep them on the move to avoid burning. Turn onto a plate to cool. Grind to a powder using a spice grinder or mortar and pestle. Sift the ground coriander into a bowl, discarding the debris.

5 Combine half the ground coriander with the oils, salt and a few grinds of pepper, then add the vinegar. Taste and add more coriander as required to develop the flavour fully.

6 Combine the carrot, sugar snaps and celeriac or celery with most of the vinaigrette and toss well. Scatter 6 side plates, shallow bowls or a platter with the witlof leaves and place the vegetables on top so that the witlof is visible. Dress with more vinaigrette [take care that the salad is not too wet], then scatter with the nuts and any remaining ground coriander, and top with the snipped mustard cress.

400g baby green beans, tops snapped off [leave the tails on]

2 Lebanese cucumbers, washed and cut into tiny dice

150g snow peas [mange-tout], washed, strings removed, cut into very fine julienne

1–2 tablespoons small oregano leaves

finely grated zest of 1 lemon

½–1 teaspoon freshly ground Sichuan pepper

20ml olive oil

30ml vegetable oil

1 teaspoon light soy sauce, or to taste

2 tablespoons toasted ground rice*

Serves 6

Salad of Baby Green Beans, Cucumber & Snow Peas

Serve this salad with deep-fried fish such as flathead or grilled swordfish [see opposite] and a tartare sauce, made by simply combining chopped parsley, tarragon, chives, eschalots and cornichons* with a thick Mayonnaise,* which is then seasoned to taste and finished with a little white-wine vinegar.

Texture is the feature of this salad and its freshness provides a good contrast to the richness of the fish.

1   Steam the beans over a pan of simmering water, keeping them slightly underdone [or cook them in plenty of well-salted boiling water]. Refresh under cold running water and drain well.

2   Combine the beans, cucumber, snow peas, oregano and lemon zest in a mixing bowl.

3   Toast the Sichuan pepper in a dry frying pan over low–medium heat until aromatic, taking care to keep it on the move to avoid burning.

4   Mix the pepper, oils and soy sauce, then taste; add more soy to achieve the saltiness that suits your palate. Pour over the vegetables and toss gently.

5   Transfer the salad to a wide shallow bowl or platter and scatter with the ground rice, then serve.

100g blanched almonds, splintered or roughly chopped

4–6 Roma tomatoes, washed and cut lengthwise into 4–6 wedges [depending on size]

sea salt [preferably Halen Môn* smoked salt]

200g snow peas [mange-tout], washed, strings removed, cut on the diagonal into 5mm-thick slices

10cm piece daikon, peeled, or 6 red radishes, washed and thinly sliced

1 large red pepper, washed, top, seeds and white membrane removed, cut into 3mm dice

1 stalk celery, washed, sliced in half crosswise, then cut into 5mm-thick pieces

6 pale inner celery leaves, washed and torn

40ml extra virgin olive oil [preferably a peppery-tasting one]

40ml vegetable oil

20ml lime juice, or to taste

freshly ground white pepper

50g Pecorino Romano or hard goat's cheese, finely shaved with a vegetable peeler

Serves 6

Salad of Tomatoes, Snow Peas, Daikon & Red Pepper with Toasted Almonds

Here is a handsome and flavoursome salad to add to a buffet table or to accompany a roast chicken served at room temperature with Mayonnaise.* The celery leaves add a hint of bitterness to the salad. A simple green salad and some good bread will complete an enjoyable summer lunch.

1 Preheat the oven to 150°C. Place the almonds on a baking tray and toast for 10 minutes or until light golden. Set aside.

2 Put the tomato in a colander and sprinkle with some salt, then leave to drain for 10 minutes or so. Pat dry with paper towel before the salad is combined.

3 Put the snow peas in a large mixing bowl.

4 Use a vegetable peeler to shave thin slices from the daikon, then cut into julienne and add to the snow peas.

5 Add the tomato, pepper, celery and celery leaves to the snow peas and daikon.

6 Combine the oils and lime juice, season to taste, then add to the vegetables and toss gently. Place on a suitably sized platter, then scatter with the almonds and shaved cheese and serve.

24–30 baby carrots, lightly scrubbed, tops trimmed [leave a little of the tops intact]

1 teaspoon caster sugar

½ teaspoon sea salt and some freshly ground white pepper

mineral water [such as Vichy] or tap water, to just cover the carrots

2 heads baby fennel, bases and tops trimmed [reserve any fronds that look fresh]

juice of ½ lemon

1 large handful sorrel leaves, bitter stalks removed, washed and patted dry

2 large handfuls very small watercress sprigs, washed and spin-dried

Vinaigrette

1 small clove garlic, smashed

100ml extra virgin olive oil

20ml verjuice*

20ml lemon juice, or to taste

sea salt and freshly ground pepper

Serves 6

Baby Carrot & Shaved Fennel Salad with Sorrel & Watercress

The sweetness of carrots sits well with the aromatic fresh flavour of fennel. Sorrel has a strident lemony acidity and the watercress provides a slightly piquant balance to this dish. Serve with roast veal, shallow-fried veal escalopes or grilled lamb cutlets [see opposite].

1 Select a shallow saucepan with a tight-fitting lid that will hold the carrots without too much space above them. Put in the carrots, sugar, salt, a little pepper and mineral water or water and bring to the boil over high heat. Reduce the heat to low and simmer, covered, for 4–5 minutes, then check for tenderness. They may take more time; don't let them become too soft as this salad is about firm textures.

2 Using a sharp knife or mandoline,* thinly shave the fennel into a large mixing bowl and toss with the lemon juice.

3 To make the vinaigrette, rub a small mixing bowl with the garlic and discard the debris. Add the olive oil, verjuice, lemon juice, salt and pepper, combine well, and then add the fennel fronds.

4 Drain the fennel, then moisten it with half the vinaigrette. Arrange the carrots neatly in a shallow bowl, then moisten it with the remaining vinaigrette and add the fennel.

5 Roll the sorrel leaves into a cigar shape and shave thinly with a very sharp knife. Scatter the sorrel and watercress over the salad and serve.

Poached Lambs' Brains with Carrot Salad and a Creamy Dressing

For a delicious entrée salad for those who enjoy offal try this variation. Clean, poach and slice lambs' brains. Replace the vinaigrette I've given here with one made by whisking together 2 teaspoons Dijon mustard, 40ml crème fraîche,* 80ml extra virgin olive oil and lemon juice, salt and pepper to taste. Moisten the fennel and carrots with a little of this vinaigrette, scatter with sorrel, then place the brains on top. Coat them with the vinaigrette, then scatter with some finely chopped curly-leaf parsley and garnish with watercress sprigs.

1 large organic eggplant [aubergine], peeled	**Dressing**
2 teaspoons sea salt	60ml organic brown rice vinegar [Spiral brand]
1 tablespoon finely sliced organic spring onions	40ml shao hsing wine or dry sherry
40ml organic extra virgin olive oil	3 cloves organic garlic, finely diced
	1 tablespoon finely diced organic ginger
	1 tablespoon brown sugar
	20ml organic tamari [Spiral brand]
	½ teaspoon organic sesame oil [Spiral brand]
	Serves 4

Kylie Kwong's Chinese-style Eggplant Salad

Australia is very fortunate to have so many brilliant young chefs working across a broad range of cuisines. Not the least of these is my fine friend Kylie Kwong, whose Sydney restaurant, Billy Kwong, is a triumphant celebration of her own style of creative and traditional Chinese cooking. Here is a delicious recipe in Kylie's words that encapsulates her unique style – thank you, Kylie.

1   Cut the eggplant lengthwise into 15mm slices then cut each slice into 15mm strips. Sprinkle the eggplant with salt on both sides and lay on a tray in one layer. Set aside for 10 minutes.

2   Meanwhile, to make the dressing, place all the ingredients in a small heavy-based saucepan and bring to the boil. Reduce the heat and simmer, uncovered, for 2 minutes or until slightly reduced, then set aside.

3   Place the eggplant in a colander and rinse well under cold running water. Drain and pat dry with paper towel.

4   Arrange the eggplant in one layer on a heatproof plate that will fit inside a steamer basket. Place the plate inside the steamer, position it over a deep saucepan or wok of boiling water and steam, covered, for 6 minutes or until the eggplant is just tender when pierced with a knife. Carefully remove the plate from the steamer and allow the eggplant to cool slightly.

5   To serve, arrange the eggplant on a platter and spoon over the reserved dressing. Sprinkle with spring onion and drizzle with extra virgin olive oil.

1.2kg black mussels, cleaned

1 clove garlic, smashed

1 bay leaf

a few sprigs thyme

a splash dry vermouth or dry white wine

350g small Swiss Brown mushrooms or button mushrooms, stalks trimmed and caps thinly sliced

¼ cup roughly chopped curly-leaf parsley

1–2 crisp eating apples

40–60ml verjuice*

freshly ground white pepper

cos lettuce leaves, washed and spin-dried, to serve

Vinaigrette

1 clove garlic, any green shoot removed, finely chopped

1 teaspoon thyme leaves

2–3 tablespoons double cream

a splash cider, seaweed, eschalot and fleur de sel vinegar*

finely grated zest of ½ lemon

freshly ground white pepper

Serves 6

Mussel, Mushroom & Apple Salad

This simple melange of ingredients matches nicely with fish such as grilled ocean trout fillets or barramundi cutlets. Place the salad in two stacked baby cos leaves to provide a textural element. Alternatively, use the salad to moisten steamed and carefully skinned baby John Dory. Scrape away the little bones around the sides of each John Dory, then serve this dish at room temperature. Ideal as a main course on a hot day.

1 Select a deep, wide-based frying pan that has a tight-fitting lid. Cook the mussels in 4 batches, since overloading the pan means that some of the mussels will probably overcook. Put a layer of mussels into the pan with a quarter of the garlic, bay leaf and thyme, then add a splash of vermouth or white wine. Cover the pan and place over the highest heat possible, then shake from time to time while holding the lid on tightly; look for a whisper of steam emanating from the side of the lid. Lift off the lid and, the second the mussels open, transfer them to a large bowl, using tongs. Strain the liquid through a sieve lined with moistened muslin cloth or paper towel and set aside; you will need a tablespoon or so for the vinaigrette. Repeat this process until all the mussels have opened, discarding the odd ones that refuse to cooperate. Remove the mussels from the shells and set aside.

2 Combine the mussels, mushrooms and parsley in a mixing bowl.

3 To make the vinaigrette, whisk together the ingredients plus 20ml of the reserved mussel liquor, seasoning with pepper only [the mussel juice is very salty]. Use to dress the mussels and mushrooms.

4 Core and halve the apples but don't peel them. Cut them into small dice, then toss in verjuice and set aside for 5 minutes. Drain well and toss with the other ingredients, then season to taste with pepper.

5 If the salad is too wet, use a slotted spoon to transfer it into the cos leaves. [This won't be necessary if serving this salad with John Dory or another fish.] Serve immediately.

2 salad onions

sea salt and freshly ground white pepper

5 Lebanese cucumbers, peeled, cut into 2mm-thick slices

ice cubes

300g fresh firm ricotta [preferably buffalo ricotta]

1 clove garlic, any green shoot removed, very finely chopped

150g light sour cream or crème fraîche*

¼–⅓ cup lightly chopped dill

Serves 6–8

Stephanie Puharich's Cucumber & Ricotta Salad

This recipe is from the mother of my butcher, Anthony Puharich of Vic's Premium Quality Meats and Victor Churchill.* Stephanie developed her passion for cooking as a young girl after the family decided she was more of a hindrance doing her share of farm chores than she might be staying indoors. Picking up a recipe book that happened to be lying around, she began by baking a cherry cake that took her fancy. The result was so successful that it established her role as the family's cook. Stephanie's passion for cooking is still as strong today, some forty-five years on. This is a recipe Stephanie remembers from her childhood growing up in the central region of Croatia. Her mother would serve it in summer as an accompaniment to grilled fish or meat. I guess the onions came from the vegetable garden and the cheese was homemade. The salad presents well in a rustic pottery bowl.

Thank you, Stephanie, for contributing this unique example of Croatian country-style cooking.

1 Trim off the root and peel the outer layer off the onions. Discard any damaged part of the green tops. Cut the bulbs and all the green tops into 5mm-thick slices, then drop them into a saucepan of cold water and bring to the boil. Drain and refresh under cold running water. Drain again and dry thoroughly with paper towel, then transfer to a large bowl and season with salt and pepper.

2 Put the cucumber into a bowl containing plenty of ice cubes and water to cover them, then leave for 20 minutes. Drain well and dry thoroughly with paper towel. This technique renders the cucumbers super-crisp.

3 Cream the ricotta in a food processor, pulsing it just enough to make it smooth. Transfer to a bowl [using the processor to add the sour cream may cause the mixture to curdle] and combine with the garlic and sour cream until smooth, then season to taste.

4 Using a large metal spoon, fold the onion, cucumber and dill into the cheese mixture, then taste and adjust the seasoning. Cover and refrigerate for about 2 hours to allow the flavours to develop.

300g wild rice	
1.5 litres water	
sea salt	
40ml verjuice*	
2 pale inner stalks celery, leaves roughly chopped and stalks finely diced [to yield about 1 cup chopped stalks]	
2 firm ripe pears, washed, cored and cut into 5mm dice	
4 pieces preserved lemon, flesh discarded, rind finely chopped	

Walnut pesto

100g walnut kernels
1 clove garlic, any green shoot removed, roughly chopped
½ teaspoon sea salt
2 handfuls basil leaves
¼–⅓ cup finely grated Parmigiano Reggiano
80ml extra virgin olive oil
20ml walnut oil
freshly ground white pepper
40ml verjuice*
Serves 6

Wild Rice & Walnut Pesto Salad

Wild rice is not really rice, rather a cereal that looks something like brown rice. It has a nutty, sightly smoky flavour and is considered something of a delicacy. Wild rice is cultivated in the Mississippi Valley of the USA, Africa, South-East Asia and China, as well as Italy. The cooking method is much the same as that used for long-grain rice but when cooked it lacks the starchy quality of rice. I like to serve wild rice with grilled guinea fowl and roast quail, where its nutty character marries harmoniously.

This salad employs the subtle flavour of a walnut-based pesto that uses less garlic and blends well with the wild rice. Celery provides a fresh texture and flavour that is contrasted by the natural sweetness of the pears and some acidity from the preserved lemon rind. The dish presents well with its delicate shades of contrasting colours. Remember this salad when looking for an accompaniment for roast turkey at Christmas.

I like to peel the walnuts of all skin for the pesto. This rids the nuts of any bitterness, so I recommend doing it the day before making the pesto.

1 Preheat the oven to 150°C. To start preparing the pesto, drop the walnuts into a small saucepan of boiling water for 1 minute, then drain. Rub as much skin as practicable off the kernels without being too fussy. Put them into the warm oven to dry out for 5 minutes; don't let them take on any colour.

2 Put the wild rice in a 3-litre capacity saucepan, cover with the cold water, then add ½ teaspoon salt and the verjuice. Bring to the boil and simmer very slowly over low heat for 40 minutes. The rice may burst if the cooking is too fast so keep an eye on it.

3 Place the cooled walnuts and remaining pesto ingredients, except the verjuice, in a food processor and work into a smooth moist paste. Check the seasoning and dilute with the verjuice. If the pesto is still on the thick side, dilute with a little water.

4 Drain the rice well in a colander, then transfer to a large mixing bowl. Gently fold the pesto into the hot rice, along with the celery and pear, then adjust the seasoning to taste.

5 Scatter with the preserved lemon and serve at room temperature or chilled.

2 small white onions, 1 peeled and 1 finely diced

sea salt

900g fresh pea pods, shelled [retain 12 empty pods]

500ml light chicken stock, well salted

100ml water

40ml extra virgin olive oil

220g vialone nano risotto rice

40ml dry white wine

Parmigiano Reggiano, very thinly shaved, to garnish

freshly ground white pepper

Vinaigrette

80ml extra virgin olive oil

20ml aged white-wine vinegar [such as Forum Chardonnay vinegar*], or to taste

sea salt and freshly ground white pepper

Serves 6

Salad of Rice & Green Peas
Insalata 'Risi e Bisi'

Risi e bisi is a type of risotto and a Venetian specialty. This simple salad is a take on that lovely dish. Serve it as part of an antipasto selection or as a salad with other dishes for a casual summer lunch, preferably outdoors where food often tastes more exciting.

1 Preheat the oven to 110°C. Bring a saucepan with plenty of water and the whole onion to the boil, then season on the salty side. Add the peas and pods and cook for 3–8 minutes or until tender but certainly not soft. Drain in a colander and refresh under cold running water, then drain very well. Discard the onion and pods [which have done their job of enriching the flavour of the peas].

2 Bring the combined chicken stock and water to the boil in a saucepan, then keep warm. Select an ovenproof saucepan with a tight-fitting lid that will hold the rice and water. Heat the oil in the pan over medium heat and cook the diced onion for 5 minutes or until translucent, then add the rice and stir over low heat until the grains reach about blood temperature and appear transparent. Add the wine and let it bubble to almost nothing. Add the hot stock mixture, stir to combine, then cover with the lid and transfer to the oven for 12 minutes.

3 Check the rice; it should be al dente and rather wet. Drain immediately into a colander and leave to cool to room temperature.

4 To make the vinaigrette, combine the olive oil and vinegar, then season to taste.

5 When the rice has cooled to room temperature, fold in the peas and the whisked vinaigrette, then transfer to a salad platter or bowl. Scatter with the shaved parmesan and coarsely grind over some pepper before serving.

12–18 baby beetroot [depending on size] with 2cm stalks attached, scrubbed

450g baby green beans, tops snapped off [leave the tails on]

sea salt

3 pale inner stalks celery, washed and cut into 4cm-long matchsticks

½ cup pale celery leaves, torn into small pieces

freshly ground white pepper

2 large handfuls small rocket sprigs, washed and spin-dried

Horseradish and walnut cream

120ml crème fraîche* or thickened cream

60g walnut kernels, finely chopped

2 tablespoons freshly grated horseradish* [or prepared horseradish* such as Tracklements brand]

sea salt and freshly ground white pepper

a little lemon juice [optional]

Serves 6

Baby Beetroot, Green Bean & Celery Salad with Horseradish & Walnut Cream

The sweet earthy flavour of the beetroot and slight bitterness of the celery are handsomely matched by the horseradish* and walnut cream dressing, which is inspired by a sauce by the master chef August Escoffier. Serve this salad as a buffet item or with crumbed pork cutlets, cold roast pork or pan-roasted barramundi. If you have access to fresh young nasturtium leaves use them with or in place of the rocket. They will add a wonderful peppery tang to this salad.

1 Preheat the oven to 180°C. Wrap each beetroot in foil and bake for 30 minutes or until they offer no resistance when pierced with a fine skewer. Cool briefly, then remove the foil, along with the skin and stalk.

2 Plunge the beans into a saucepan of boiling well-salted water and cook for 3–5 minutes or until very slightly underdone, then drain and refresh under cold running water. Drain well in a colander.

3 To make the horseradish and walnut cream, very lightly whip the crème fraîche or cream to give it some body. Combine the walnut pieces, horseradish and cream in a mixing bowl, then season to taste with salt and pepper. If needed, add a touch of lemon juice; try to avoid doing this since it is inclined to stiffen the cream, making it difficult to pour over the vegetables. Should the sauce be too thick, dilute it with a little cold water just before dressing the salad.

4 Place the beetroot and beans in separate bowls and moisten with some of the walnut cream, then toss with your hands. Arrange the beetroot and beans on a large platter, scatter with the celery and celery leaves and drizzle with the remaining walnut cream, then season with pepper. Scatter with the rocket and serve.

400g brown rice, washed in a large bowl of cold water [loose husks that come to the surface skimmed off]

2 teaspoons fine sea salt

2.4 litres water

8–10 spring onions, trimmed and thinly sliced, keeping the green parts separate

1 red pepper, finely diced

1 green pepper, finely diced

2 inner pale stalks celery, including some leaves, finely sliced

80g dried sultanas

1 cup roughly chopped flat-leaf parsley

100g pecan nuts, walnut kernels or blanched almonds, chopped and toasted in a dry pan

sea salt and freshly ground black pepper

freshly grated nutmeg, to taste

Walnut vinaigrette [optional]

80ml extra virgin olive oil

30ml grapeseed oil

30ml walnut or hazelnut oil

cider vinegar* or a mixture of cider vinegar and lemon juice, to taste

sea salt and freshly ground black pepper

Sesame vinaigrette [optional]

120ml grapeseed oil

40ml sesame oil

20–40ml rice vinegar

soy sauce, to taste

freshly ground white pepper or chopped chilli to taste

Serves 6–8

Brown Rice Salad

Unmilled rice is a highly nutritious food due to the retention of the outer layers or husks, which provide an excellent source of dietary fibre. Naturally it requires longer cooking and should retain a slightly crunchy texture. As opposed to the relative blandness of white [or polished] rice, brown rice has a robust nutty flavour and can be made into delicious salads using a wide range of other ingredients such as raw vegetables, cooked meat, poultry and fish.

Use this recipe as a base then experiment with other ingredients to expand your repertoire, bearing in mind the optional sesame vinaigrette. Alternative ingredients that work well with brown rice include: apples; white onions; pine nuts; finely shredded witlof and radicchio; mushrooms; small quantities of fresh sage; radishes; daikon; avocado; cauliflower; broccoli; tomatoes; ham; cooked game [such as quail]; turkey; chicken; leftover roast leg of lamb; fried pancetta; flaked cooked flathead or barramundi; crabmeat; and prawns. So be creative and keep in mind achieving a balance between acidic, sweet and salty ingredients.

1 Bring the rice, salt and water slowly to the boil in a large saucepan and cook as directed on the packet. Drain in a colander and cool to room temperature. Season with salt, pepper and nutmeg.

2 Choose one of the vinaigrettes and whisk the ingredients to combine.

3 Put the rice in a mixing bowl, then add the spring onion, peppers, celery, sultanas, parsley and nuts. Moisten with the vinaigrette and toss thoroughly, using your hands. Scatter with the sliced green spring onions and serve in a wide salad bowl.

1 head fennel with some fronds attached, tops and bases trimmed, outer coarse ribs removed, cut into eighths lengthwise

2 large Lebanese cucumbers, peeled and cut into 2cm dice

1 large firm avocado,* peeled, seeded and cut into 1cm dice

1 handful flat-leaf parsley leaves, washed and spin-dried, roughly shredded

2 teaspoons walnut oil or pistachio oil

20ml extra virgin olive oil

40ml olive oil or vegetable oil

20ml cider vinegar,* or to taste

1 eschalot, finely diced

sea salt and freshly ground white pepper

12 small cos lettuce leaves, washed and spin-dried

1 × 100g jar ocean trout roe or freshwater trout roe

Serves 6

Salad of Fennel, Cucumber & Avocado with Ocean Trout Roe

This salad is best enjoyed in the cos leaves [see opposite], as this allows the flavours and textures to come together as one. Serve with grilled ocean trout or tuna fillets or king prawns cooked in their shells on the barbecue.

1 Shave the fennel into 2mm-thick slices using a sharp knife or a mandoline* and put in a mixing bowl.

2 Add the cucumber, avocado and parsley to the fennel. Combine the oils, vinegar and eschalot, then season with salt and pepper and adjust with vinegar so the vinaigrette tastes slightly sharp. Moisten the vegetables with most of the vinaigrette [taking care not to over-moisten them] and toss gently.

3 Distribute the salad between the cos leaves, then top with the roe and serve.

2 Lebanese cucumbers, washed and dried with paper towel

ice cubes

2 small blood oranges or 1 orange

2 cloves garlic, green shoot removed, smashed

a small pinch sea salt

40ml extra virgin olive oil

18 × 7mm-thick slices baguette

2 large handfuls small watercress sprigs, washed and spin-dried

freshly ground black pepper

Vinaigrette

30ml vino cotto* or fig vino cotto,* or to taste

30ml extra virgin olive oil

Serves 6

Watercress, Cucumber &
Orange Salad with Garlic Croûtons

This salad is a suitable accompaniment for grilled tuna or swordfish fillets or pan-fried veal loin steaks, topped with a dessertspoonful of pesto [see page 28]. It is also good with butterflied quail grilled with Provençale herbs and olive oil. Vino cotto is made from the must [unfermented juice] left after pressing wine grapes, which is then reduced to a syrupy consistency. It has an enormous amount of flavour and may be diluted with olive oil or a touch of water. Vino cotto is also available flavoured with figs and other fruits.

1 Preheat the oven to 150°C. Using a strong table fork, score the cucumber skins along their lengths in fairly straight lines, then cut them into 3mm-thick slices. Transfer to a bowl of very cold water with 1 handful ice cubes and leave for 20 minutes or so. This technique will produce very crisp slices.

2 Using a very sharp paring knife, cut a thin slice crosswise from the top and bottom of the oranges. Place a cut surface on a board and allow the knife to follow the contour of the fruit between the flesh and pith; take your time and aim for a smoothly rounded finish. Now hold the orange in one hand over a strainer set on a bowl so as to collect the fruit and juice. Slice between the pith and flesh to produce fillets that will fall into the strainer below. Cut each fillet into 2–3 pieces. This may be done ahead of time.

3 Using the flat side of a knife on a chopping board, work the garlic and a pinch of salt into a paste, then transfer to a bowl with the olive oil and mix together. Use a teaspoon to spread this paste over one side of each baguette slice, then tear each one into 3–4 pieces. Place on a baking tray and bake for 5 minutes or until lightly coloured but not hard.

4 Drain the cucumber, then carefully dry with a clean cloth or paper towel. Put the orange, cucumber and watercress in a salad bowl.

5 To make the vinaigrette, combine the vino cotto and olive oil.

6 Moisten the ingredients in the salad bowl with the vinaigrette, then toss lightly. Grind pepper over the salad at the last minute. Serve scattered with the warm garlic croûtons.

Special Occasion Salads

Salades de fête

1 head celeriac [about 400g]	

1 large King Brown mushroom, cut into julienne

3 small ripe but slightly firm avocados*

3–4 firm ripe tomatoes* [such as Love Bites or Romas], peeled, seeded and cut into 5mm dice

1 handful frisée lettuce, cut into tiny tufts, or mâche lettuce, washed and spin-dried

Truffle mayonnaise

1 × 30g fresh or frozen truffle

3 eggs

½ teaspoon sea salt

freshly ground white pepper

1 teaspoon Dijon mustard

40ml extra virgin olive oil

80ml grapeseed oil

20ml hazelnut oil

10–20ml aged sherry vinegar or best quality cider vinegar*

2 drops truffle oil [optional]

Serves 6 as a starter

Truffled Celeriac & Mushroom Salad

Here is an extravagant salad for a celebratory dinner that need not break the bank. Your guests will be thrilled by its flavour and presentation. You will need to start two days ahead of time.

1   To start to prepare the mayonnaise, put the truffle and whole eggs in a container with a tight-fitting lid and seal, then refrigerate for 2 days before you wish to serve.

2   On the day the salad is to be served, prick 1 of the eggs with a fine pin and lower it into a saucepan of boiling water, then boil for 10 minutes. Drain and refresh it under cold running water. Shell the egg, then cut in half and drop the yolk into a small mixing bowl and mash using a fork.

3   Separate the remaining eggs, adding the yolks to the bowl [keep the whites for an omelette, see page 140] with the salt, some pepper and the mustard, then whisk to combine. Slowly add the combined oils in a fine stream, whisking continuously and taking care not to add more oil before the previous addition is absorbed. Continue adding the remaining oil until quite thick, then acidulate with vinegar and adjust seasoning to taste. The texture should be thick enough to coat the salad ingredients. Only add the truffle oil if a boost of flavour is required; too much results in an artificial taste.

4   Using a very sharp chef's knife or a mandoline,* cut the celeriac into 2mm-thick slices, then cut these into 2mm-thick julienne with a knife. Cut the truffle into 2mm-thick slices, then into 2mm-thick julienne. Cover separately with plastic film.

5   Put 2–3 tablespoons of the truffle mayonnaise into a large mixing bowl, then add the celeriac and mushroom, adding just enough of the mayonnaise to hold them together. The texture should be moist yet stiff enough to hold its weight. Cover closely with a piece of plastic film, then seal the bowl. It is better to do this an hour or so before serving so that the truffle flavour mingles with the vegetables.

6   Cut the avocados in half lengthwise, then working one at a time, hold the half with the stone still attached in one hand, tap the stone with a sharp knife and twist gently to remove it. Cut each avocado half into quarters, then place on a chopping board. This may be done ahead of time provided each piece is tightly covered with plastic film to prevent discolouration.

7   Cut each avocado quarter in half lengthwise, then crosswise into 2mm-thick slices and arrange on one side of 6 entrée plates. Place a tall pile of the celeriac and mushroom mixture in the centre of each plate. Add the tomato, then garnish with frisée or mâche and serve immediately.

2 red peppers

2 bunches sorrel, stalks removed, leaves washed at the last minute and patted dry

1 small clove garlic, finely chopped

20ml Noilly Prat vermouth or dry white wine

sea salt and freshly ground white pepper

20ml double cream

50g hazelnut kernels

12 × 4cm × 1.5cm × 5mm-thick croûtons cut from Vienna-style bread or brioche

extra virgin olive oil

36 scallops [with roe if possible]

2 heads small red witlof, leaves separated, trimmed to half their length

2 small heads white witlof [or the inner leaves of larger ones], leaves separated, trimmed to half their length

Vinaigrette

60ml hazelnut oil

40ml grapeseed oil

2–3 teaspoons cider, seaweed, eschalot and fleur de sel vinegar,* or to taste

sea salt and freshly ground white pepper

Serves 6 as an entrée

Warm Salad of Scallops, Sorrel Croûtons & Grilled Red Pepper with Witlof

The sweet flavour of scallops is complemented by the acidity of sorrel, robust sweetness of grilled pepper and slight bitterness of witlof. The palate of this salad is brought together by a hazelnut vinaigrette. I recommend buying scallops with the roe attached, if possible, for the best flavour. Sourdough bread is likely to dry out so use a Vienna-style loaf or brioche. An elegant entrée for formal dining.

1 Preheat the oven to 160°C. Grill the peppers over a direct gas flame or on a cast-iron chargrill until blackened. Transfer to a plate and seal with plastic film for 15 minutes. Peel off the skins with your fingertips and with the aid of a paring knife. Don't be tempted to wash off the skin since this will spoil the flavour. Slice off the tops and bottoms then cut in halves lengthwise and remove the seeds and membrane, then cut into very thin matchsticks.

2 Place the sorrel, garlic and vermouth in a saucepan, season lightly with salt and pepper, then cover the pan and cook over low–medium heat, stirring occasionally, until the sorrel has collapsed to a moist purée. Increase the heat to evaporate the liquid, then add the cream. Adjust the seasoning, turn onto a plate and cover with plastic film.

3 Place the hazelnuts in a small ovenproof frying pan and toast in the oven until the skins split. Turn immediately into a sieve and use a clean tea towel to rub them against the sieve; this will remove most of the skins. Return to the oven and toast again; watch carefully since they burn easily. Turn onto a plate to cool, then chop very finely.

4 Reduce the oven temperature to 150°C. Paint the croûtons lightly with olive oil and toast in the oven until pale golden, keeping a close eye on them to ensure they don't dry out and become hard.

5 To make the vinaigrette, whisk the hazelnut and grapeseed oils with the vinegar and season to taste with salt and pepper. Put most of the vinaigrette into a good-sized bowl.

6 Pick over each scallop, trimming and discarding the hard tissue. Trim off the scallop roe and set aside.

7 Heat a heavy-based frying pan over high heat to near smoking temperature. Season the scallops, then add a very little olive oil to the pan and sear the scallops in batches. They should gain some colour but remain raw inside. Transfer the scallops to the vinaigrette as they are cooked, tossing immediately so that the flavours mingle.

8 Distribute the witlof and peppers between 6 entrée plates, spread the sorrel on the croûtons, then place 2 on each plate. Put the scallops on the croûtons, then dust them with hazelnuts. Add the remaining hazelnuts to the juices in the bowl and use to moisten the leaves and peppers. Serve at once.

2 large handfuls mixed salad leaves, washed and spin-dried

6 small button mushrooms, stalks removed, caps thinly sliced

Omelette

1 × 20g fresh or frozen truffle

6 eggs

40ml crème fraîche* or pouring cream

2 tablespoons chopped curly-leaf parsley [optional]

sea salt and freshly ground white pepper

40g clarified butter*

Vinaigrette

40ml extra virgin olive oil

2 teaspoons aged sherry vinegar or aged red-wine vinegar [such as Forum Cabernet vinegar*]

sea salt and freshly ground white or black pepper

Serves 2

A Truffled Salad & Omelette for Two

This is perfect food for a romantic supper after a show. A twenty-gram truffle will be plenty for two people. You will need to put the truffle in with the eggs two days in advance so that their fragrance infuses the eggs, then prepare the leaves and truffles before going to the theatre. The remaining ingredients can be assembled in a few minutes.

1 To start preparing the omelette, put the truffle and eggs in a container with a tight-fitting lid, then seal and refrigerate 2 days before you wish to serve.

2 A few hours before cooking, break the eggs into a bowl. Cut the truffle into fine julienne, then add one-quarter to the eggs. Cover with plastic film and refrigerate. Put the remaining truffle and vinaigrette ingredients on a tray, then seal with plastic film.

3 When ready to cook the omelette, have your partner shake the vinaigrette ingredients in a screw-top jar and put the salad leaves and mushrooms in a salad bowl.

4 Use a fork to break the eggs and lightly combine with the truffle, crème fraîche and parsley, if using; don't beat the mixture. Season and taste to be sure it is right for salt.

5 Heat a 24–26cm frying pan over high heat and drop in the butter, allowing it to melt and get really hot [but not smoking]. Immediately pour in the egg mixture.

6 Wait a moment for the egg mixture to set, then shake the pan and tilt it down, using a fork or spatula to draw the cooked egg away from the edge of the pan to allow the raw mixture to flow underneath and cook; don't let the omelette become dry.

7 Gather half the omelette to one side of the pan [preferably opposite the handle], making a crescent shape in the middle so that it will turn out of the pan the same shape as the rounded edge. The cooking time should be 70–80 seconds.

8 Hold a gently warmed plate in one hand on a slight angle. Holding the pan handle from underneath on a similar angle, tip your omelette slowly onto the plate. I suggest you test the omelette and develop your skills without the truffles; just be patient and concentrate and the technique will be with you forever.

9 Toss the salad with the vinaigrette and remaining truffle, then serve with the omelette.

110g hazelnut kernels	**Poached quail eggs**
2–3 red peppers	a few drops white-wine vinegar
3 handfuls mixed salad leaves [including tiny watercress and frisée lettuce sprigs], washed and spin-dried	24 quail eggs, at fridge temperature
	ice cubes
1 tablespoon thyme leaves	**Vinaigrette**
4 cornichons,* thinly sliced	1 clove garlic, smashed
4 tablespoons finely diced celery	2 tablespoons reserved toasted hazelnut kernels
8 medium-sized mushrooms, stalks trimmed, caps thinly sliced	20ml hazelnut oil
	40ml grapeseed oil
½ × 180g jar foie gras* [such as Rougié brand]	2 teaspoons verjuice*
boiling water, for dipping	2 teaspoons aged sherry vinegar or cider vinegar*
	sea salt and freshly ground white pepper
	Serves 6

Salad of Quail Eggs, Red Peppers & Toasted Hazelnuts with Foie Gras

Quail eggs have a delicate, slightly acidic flavour that sits happily with the sweetness of the grilled red peppers. Toasted hazelnuts and foie gras enrich the leaves, while a little celery adds a touch of bitterness. If preferred, slices of briskly fried chicken livers may be substituted for the foie gras.

1 Preheat the oven to 160°C. Toast the hazelnuts in the oven for 10 minutes or until the skins split. Tip them into a coarse sieve and rub off the skins with a clean tea towel; don't be too fussy about a few bits remaining. Put 2 tablespoons aside for the vinaigrette, then roughly chop the rest. Return to the oven and toast briefly to give them some colour.

2 Grill the peppers over an open gas flame [or better still on a barbecue] until blackened. Put in a freezer bag for 15 minutes. Peel the peppers, discarding the inner membrane and seeds, then cut into thin strips [never let grilled peppers come near water as this diminishes their flavour].

3 Place the salad leaves, thyme, cornichon, celery and mushroom in a mixing bowl, cover with plastic film, then refrigerate until required.

4 To make the vinaigrette, rub a small bowl with the garlic, then discard the debris. Grind the reserved hazelnuts to a coarse powder in a food processor using the pulse action; take care not to grind them to a paste. Whisk the oils, verjuice and vinegar, then season to taste, finishing with enough ground hazelnuts to give the vinaigrette some body.

5 Hold the jar of foie gras firmly and pull the protruding nib of the rubber seal to break the vacuum. Open the jar and dip it into near-boiling water to loosen the foie gras. Use a small paring knife to gently remove the foie gras and tip it onto a chopping board. [The leftover foie gras can be stored in the fridge and is best consumed within 2 days.]

6 To poach the eggs, bring a small frying pan of water to the boil with the vinegar. Pierce the shells with a sharp paring knife, then use scissors to open them. Slip 4 quail eggs onto dessertspoons. Have a bowl of cold water with plenty of ice cubes ready to slip the cooked eggs into to arrest the cooking; the aim is to have slightly runny yolks.

7 Slip the eggs into the simmering water and poach for a bit over 1 minute, then retrieve with a slotted spoon and drop into the icy water. Transfer the eggs one by one onto a folded clean tea towel to drain.

8 Scatter 6 entrée plates with the roasted pepper. Moisten the leaves with some vinaigrette and distribute over the peppers. Place 4 quail eggs on each plate. Cut the foie gras into strips and scatter over the salads. Moisten the eggs with vinaigrette, scatter with the chopped hazelnuts and serve immediately.

2–3 × 5mm-thick slices ciabatta bread, roughly torn into 5mm pieces

100ml light olive oil

sea salt and freshly ground white pepper

4 litres water

700g very small uncooked prawns [such as school prawns]

2 tomatoes* with good flavour [such as Ox Heart or Roma], peeled, seeded and cut into 5mm dice

10 tiny button mushrooms, stalks removed, caps cut into 3mm-thick slices

2–3 handfuls mesclun [see page xiii], washed and spin-dried

extra virgin olive oil, for drizzling

Mayonnaise

1 small clove garlic, smashed

2 egg yolks

1 heaped teaspoon Dijon mustard

¼ teaspoon sea salt

freshly ground white pepper

100ml grapeseed oil

100ml extra virgin olive oil

cider, seaweed, eschalot and fleur de sel vinegar*

Serves 6 a starter

Little Prawn Nests

A good prawn cocktail may be considered retro but it never fails to please when it makes an appearance on Bistro Moncur's menu. School prawns are tiny, delicately flavoured and sweet but take time to peel, while king prawns are often dense in texture. I like to use the smallest school prawns and cook them as briefly as possible, then let them cool at room temperature, spread out on a tray to speed up the process. For the best flavour, cook the prawns as close to serving them as possible and don't refrigerate; simply place the bowl over some ice. While thinking about prawn cocktails I decided to make it more of a salad by incorporating button mushrooms and tomatoes and spiking the mayonnaise with a wonderful cider vinegar* flavoured with seaweed, eschalot and a special salt called fleur de sel. This salad is excellent as a little starter before the principal entrée in a formal menu. If it is to be the entrée then double the quantities.

1   To make the mayonnaise, rub a small mixing bowl with the garlic and discard the debris. Whisk the egg yolks, mustard, salt and some pepper to combine. Slowly add the combined oils in a fine stream, whisking continuously and taking care not to add more oil before the previous addition is absorbed. Continue adding the remaining oil until quite thick, then acidulate with a little vinegar and adjust the seasoning. The texture should be thick enough to coat the salad ingredients.

2   Place the bread in a large bowl. Slowly drizzle 60ml of the light olive oil over the bread, tossing it to distribute the oil evenly. Season lightly with salt and pepper. Heat the remaining olive oil in a non-stick frying pan over medium heat and sauté the bread until golden; keep the pan moving to colour the bread evenly since there is so little oil. Turn into a sieve, then drain on paper towel.

3   Bring the water to the boil in a saucepan and cook the prawns in 3–4 batches for about 1 minute or less after the water returns to the boil. The prawns should have turned pink and feel just firm when gently squeezed. Use a wire lifter to transfer them to a wide bowl, then toss liberally with sea salt. Transfer the prawns to a wide tray, then spread them out so that they cool quickly.

4   Shell the cooled prawns, then moisten them with just enough of the mayonnaise to bind them with the tomato and mushroom, folding gently to combine. Use tongs to form little towers of this mixture in the centre of 6 deep entrée plates. Add the croûtons to the mesclun, then distribute around the prawns to make nests, finishing with a drizzle of extra virgin olive oil.

4–5 mustard fruits* [preferably fig mustard fruits], drained and finely shaved

180g Manchego sheep's milk cheese, crust removed, finely shaved

3 handfuls mixed salad leaves [such as torn radicchio, witlof tips, tiny baby spinach and frisée lettuce], washed and spin-dried [except the witlof]

Vinaigrette

1 clove garlic, smashed

1 teaspoon mustard fruit* syrup

60ml extra virgin olive oil [preferably a peppery-tasting one]

2 teaspoons aged sherry vinegar, or to taste

sea salt and freshly ground black pepper

Serves 6 to follow a main course

My Special Birthday Salad

My partner organised the most spectacular event to celebrate my half-century birthday, calling upon dear friends to cook lunch for thirty guests. The cast consisted of my chef at Bistro Moncur at the time, Jason Roberts, Maggie Beer and Stephanie Alexander so, as you can imagine, it was a meal not to be forgotten. Maggie's main course was a ballotine of her Barossa chicken filled with caramelised onion and sautéed blond chicken livers. Maggie served this delicious salad, with its perfectly tuned palate, using the salty Spanish cheese Manchego, sweet and spicy mustard fruits and some bitter and crisp leaves, in individual salad bowls halfway through the main course. I urge you to try it since it showcases Maggie Beer's clear understanding of how to balance flavour and texture.

1 To make the vinaigrette, rub a large mixing bowl with the garlic, then discard the debris. Whisk all the ingredients together then check the seasoning and acidity; it should have a slightly sharp finish so adjust with more vinegar if needed.

2 Add the mustard fruit and Manchego to the leaves, then moisten with the vinaigrette and toss carefully with your hands. Serve immediately.

2 × 1–1.2 kg live mudcrabs* [preferably female] or
2 cooked mudcrabs

3 firm ripe avocados*

3–4 heads small witlof, damaged outer leaves discarded

2 spring onions, white part only, peeled and finely sliced

Crisp basil leaves

120ml grapeseed oil

20 basil leaves

Vinaigrette

1 × 3cm piece ginger, peeled

50ml grapeseed oil

40ml hazelnut oil

20ml verjuice*

1 teaspoon lime juice, or to taste

sea salt and freshly ground white pepper

Serves 6–8 as an entrée

A Delicious Mudcrab Salad

Australian mudcrab is a great delicacy. Its sweet, slightly muddy flavour marries well here with the nuttiness of avocado, while a slight touch of bitterness is added in the form of witlof. The ginger-scented dressing is fresh and offers vitality to the mix. Follow this special entrée with barbecued quail seasoned with herbes de Provence,* Wild Rice Salad [see page 49] and lightly blanched asparagus finished for a moment on a ribbed cast-iron chargrill. Dessert could be as simple as sliced mangoes moistened with late-harvest semillon and freshly ground white pepper. This sounds like a great Aussie menu for a summer's day.

1   If using live mudcrabs cook them using the method in the Glossary.* Crack and pick out the flesh of the cooked crabs, then refrigerate.

2   To make the vinaigrette, grate the ginger using a ginger-grating plane or box grater placed over a plate to collect the juices. Combine 2 teaspoons grated ginger with the collected juice, both oils, verjuice and lime juice then season; it should taste fresh and zingy. Moisten the mudcrab with 40ml of the vinaigrette, folding gently.

3   Cut the avocados in half lengthwise, then, working one at a time, hold the half with the stone still attached in one hand; tap the stone with a fair-sized sharp knife, then twist the knife to release the stone. Peel the avocados and lay them on a chopping board. This may be done ahead of time provided each piece is tightly covered with plastic film to prevent discolouration.

4   Select 24 of the best looking witlof leaves and set aside. Thinly shave the remainder lengthwise. Combine the shaved witlof with the mudcrab and spring onion.

5   To make the crisp basil leaves, heat the grapeseed oil in a saucepan over medium heat until quite hot, then fry the basil leaves for 20 seconds until crisp and drain on paper towel.

6   Cut each avocado half in 2 lengthwise and place the pieces randomly on 6 flat entrée plates, close to the centre. Lay 2 pairs of witlof leaves on each plate. Distribute the mudcrab mixture evenly between the plates, then scatter with the slightly crumbled basil leaves. Drizzle any remaining vinaigrette around each salad. Serve at once.

½ cauliflower, cut into florets*	**Hazelnut crust**
extra virgin olive oil, for cooking	100g hazelnut kernels
24 scallops, the tiny hard piece on the side snipped off with a sharp knife or scissors	a trace cayenne pepper
	½ clove garlic, any green shoot removed, crushed
1 handful tiny watercress sprigs, washed and spin-dried	a tiny pinch salt
Watercress purée	25g [⅓ cup] sourdough breadcrumbs
2 litres water	2 tablespoons finely chopped curly-leaf parsley
1 clove garlic, smashed	100g soft unsalted butter, chopped into small pieces
sea salt	**Vinaigrette**
2 large bunches watercress, washed, coarse stalks discarded	30ml grapeseed oil
	40ml hazelnut oil
20ml verjuice,* or to taste	sea salt and freshly ground white pepper
2 teaspoons extra virgin olive oil	lime juice, to taste
freshly ground white pepper	**Serves 6 as an entrée**

Hazelnut-crusted Queensland Sea Scallop & Cauliflower Salad with Watercress Purée

I created this salad as part of a five-course tasting menu served at Adelaide's Windy Point Restaurant when I was invited to be their guest chef. It is simple and delicious as a second entrée served prior to a game dish such as roast squab [pigeon]. The four key flavours marry so well, a good example of less is more!

1 To make the hazelnut crust, preheat the oven to 160°C. Toast the hazelnuts for 10 minutes or until the skins split. Tip them into a coarse sieve and rub off the skins with a clean tea towel; don't be too fussy about a few bits remaining. Chop the hazelnuts and remaining crust ingredients in a food processor using the pulse function until just combined; take care not to overwork as this will release the oil from the nuts.

2 Meanwhile, soak the cauliflower in cold water for 20 minutes or so. Drain and blanch in a saucepan of boiling salted water for 1–2 minutes [from when the water returns to the boil], then drain and refresh under cold running water. Drain very well.

3 To make the vinaigrette, whisk the oils and seasoning together, then adjust with lime juice to taste fresh.

4 To make the watercress purée, bring the water to the boil with the garlic in a saucepan, then discard the garlic. Add a good pinch of salt and blanch the watercress for 3 minutes or until very soft. Drain and refresh under cold running water, then drain and squeeze almost dry. Purée in a blender with the verjuice and olive oil. Add a little of the vinaigrette, then taste and adjust the seasoning.

5 Heat a frying pan over high heat until it is searingly hot, then add a smear of olive oil and, when it begins to smoke, seal the scallops, in batches, very quickly on one side only. Transfer to a baking tray as they are seared, raw-side up. Top with the hazelnut crust mixture.

6 Preheat an overhead griller to maximum.

7 Smear the watercress purée over 6 flat entrée plates. Dress the cauliflower with vinaigrette and distribute between the plates. Garnish with watercress sprigs.

8 Place the scallops under the very hot griller for 1 minute or until the crust looks golden and crisp.

9 Place 4 scallops on the watercress purée on each plate and serve immediately.

1 × 40–50g fresh or frozen truffle	
6 eggs	
3–4 firm ripe tomatoes* [such as Love Bites or Romas], peeled, seeded and cut into 5mm-thick strips	
8–10 small Swiss Brown mushrooms, stalks removed, caps very thinly sliced	
3–4 handfuls mixed salad leaves [such as frisée lettuce, tiny watercress sprigs, witlof tips, torn rocket leaves, mâche, torn flat-leaf parsley leaves]	
1 × 180g jar foie gras* [such as Rougié brand Whole Duck Foie Gras in Aspic with Armagnac]	
boiling water, for dipping	
ice cubes	
2 litres water	
2 teaspoons white-wine vinegar	
6 French tarragon leaves, snipped	

Vinaigrette

1 clove garlic, smashed
30ml grapeseed oil
30ml hazelnut oil
20ml peanut oil or extra virgin olive oil
10ml aged sherry vinegar, or to taste
sea salt and freshly ground white pepper

Serves 6 as an entrée

Truffled Egg Salads with Foie Gras

This salad is an entrée to share with very special friends. While the truffle needs to be put with the eggs two days in advance to flavour them, there is very little work to be done when it is time to serve this treat. One small jar of foie gras is plenty to serve six to eight. A roast tarragon chicken and saffron rice pilaf would make an excellent main course and dessert might be based on cherries or berries since these will be in season when the imported truffles arrive. However, the superb truffles from Tasmania and Western Australia arrive in July so, if you are making this during the colder months, take advantage of winter fruit such as pears and quinces, perhaps in a tart.

It's worth putting a few extra eggs in with the truffle; they might be used in another dish such as an omelette [see page 140]. By the way, there are some excellent ceramic spoons available from Richmond Hill Café and Larder* in Melbourne that help to achieve a neat shape when poaching eggs. They are also available by mail order.

1 Put the truffle and eggs in a container with a tight-fitting lid 2 days before you wish to serve this and seal.

2 Cover the tomato and mushroom with plastic film, then refrigerate. Wash and spin-dry the salad leaves except the witlof.

3 To make the vinaigrette, shake the ingredients in a screw-top jar, taste and adjust the seasoning and acidity to a slightly sharp finish. Discard the garlic.

4 Open the jar of foie gras, then dip into very hot water for 30 seconds or so and slip a small paring knife around the edge of the foie gras. Give the knife a little jerk. Gently move the knife a little to and fro and the foie gras should come out. Place it on a chopping board or plate, cover with plastic film and refrigerate until required.

5 Have a bowl of iced water at the ready. Bring the 2 litres of water to the boil, add the vinegar, then, working in batches of 2 eggs at a time, poach the eggs* for just over 2 minutes over low heat. Retrieve the eggs with a slotted spoon and lower them into the iced water. When cold, lift them out onto a clean folded tea towel to drain, then trim off any loose threads of cooked eggwhite.

6 Cut the truffle into fine julienne. Using a sharp knife dipped in boiling water, slice the foie gras into 5mm-thick matchsticks.

7 Shake the vinaigrette, then put about one-third of it into a large mixing bowl, add the leaves, tarragon, tomato and mushroom, then toss gently using your hands. Distribute between 6 deep entrée plates.

8 Make a shallow space in the centre of each salad to accommodate a poached egg, then dress the egg and salad with the remaining vinaigrette; the salad should not be saturated. Scatter with the truffle and foie gras and serve immediately.

Warm Salads

Salades tièdes

4 beetroot, with 2cm stalk attached, scrubbed

40ml extra virgin olive oil

2 cloves garlic, any green shoot removed, roughly chopped

30 mixed salad leaves [such as mustard greens, rocket and radicchio], trimmed, washed and spin-dried [large leaves shredded into 2cm-wide ribbons]

sea salt and freshly ground black pepper

20ml cider vinegar*

40ml walnut oil

150g gypsy ham, skin removed, cut into 3mm-thick slices, then cut into 3cm-long julienne

Serves 6 as an entrée

A Warm Salad of Roasted Beetroot & Mixed Leaves

This salad for the winter months might be served as an entrée, with braised lamb shanks to follow – good food to warm the soul on a cold day. Roasted beetroot is delicious with spicy leaves such as mustard greens, rocket and radicchio. The addition of a julienne of ham gives a further depth to the flavour of this dish.

1 Preheat the oven 180°C. Wrap the beetroot individually in foil, then bake for 40 minutes or until tender when pierced with a fine skewer; check after 30 minutes. Be sure the beetroot are totally cooked so that they develop their full sweetness. Let them cool for a moment before removing the foil, skin and stalk.

2 Reduce the oven temperature to 80°C. Put an ovenproof salad bowl and 6 entrée plates in the oven.

3 Cut each beetroot into 8 wedges and place in the warm bowl, then cover the bowl with foil.

4 Heat the olive oil in a wok or frying pan large enough to hold the leaves over medium heat. Add the garlic and cook for a moment without allowing it to colour, then add the leaves and ½ teaspoon salt and sauté briskly until the leaves have softened. Quickly grind over some pepper and transfer to the bowl with the beetroot.

5 Discard any liquid in the pan, then add the vinegar, scraping the base to dislodge any sediment. Pour this mixture over the beetroot, then add the walnut oil and ham. Toss well and serve while hot.

3 × 500g squab, removed from the fridge and packaging 30 minutes before cooking

sea salt and freshly ground white pepper

extra virgin olive oil, for cooking

250g Slippery Jack mushrooms, stalks trimmed and any pine needles discarded, or King Brown mushrooms

1 clove garlic, finely chopped

40ml water

¼ cup chopped curly-leaf or flat-leaf parsley

smaller inner leaves of 1 butter lettuce, washed and spin-dried

1 small head red witlof, leaves separated [use only 4cm of the tips]

Vinaigrette

1 clove garlic, smashed

80ml extra virgin olive oil

20ml aged balsamic vinegar

20ml aged sherry vinegar

2 teaspoons thyme leaves, lightly chopped

freshly ground white pepper

Serves 6

Warm Salad of Roast Squab, Grilled Wild Mushrooms & Bitter Leaves

Here the delicious, livery taste of squab calls for the earthiness of real forest mushrooms, so make this salad in early autumn [or as the weather begins to warm up in late winter] as this is when you can expect to see Slippery Jacks, the Australian equivalent to the European *cêpe* or porcini mushroom. The slight bitterness of witlof leaves is softened by the delicacy of butter lettuce, while the vinaigrette is laced with the roasting juices from the squab. A superb salad for a special dinner.

1 Preheat the oven to 170° C. Fifteen minutes before roasting the squab, pat them dry with paper towel and clean out any grain lodged in the crop located at the wide end of the breast. Rub with a mixture of salt, pepper and just enough olive oil to make a wet paste.

2 For the vinaigrette, rub a small bowl with the garlic and discard the debris. Whisk the oil, vinegars and thyme leaves, then season only with pepper; it should taste slightly acidic.

3 Don't put the Slippery Jacks near water; rather use moistened paper towel to clean away any dirt. Cut into 5mm-thick slices.

4 Heat 20–40ml olive oil in a heavy-based ovenproof frying pan over low heat and gently brown the squab on all sides. Transfer to the oven and roast for 3 minutes on each breast and then breast-side up for 3–4 minutes. Remove from the oven, then pour off the cooking oil. Place the squab breast-side down in a bowl, supported by sufficient crumpled foil. Loosely cover with more foil and set aside to rest while cooking the mushrooms.

5 Heat 20–40ml olive oil in another heavy-based frying pan over high heat until it just begins to smoke. Add the mushrooms, salt and pepper and sauté rapidly over medium heat until they have softened. Reduce the heat to low, then add the garlic and sauté for another minute. Transfer to a warmed mixing bowl and seal with plastic film to retain the heat.

6 Using a medium-sized sharp knife, make an incision between each squab leg and breast, then ease away the legs, pulling them away from the carcass. Cut the legs through the joint, then transfer them to a plate. Run the knife on either side of the breastbone and cut through the wing joint, then carefully pull the breast away from the carcass. The flesh should be pink and very juicy. Carve each breast on the diagonal from the wing-end to produce about 6 slices per breast. Add to the mushrooms.

7 Add the water to the roasting sediment in the pan and reduce quickly over high heat, scraping up the sediment; this will probably be quite salty [hence the absence of salt in the vinaigrette]. Add as much of this reduction as possible to the vinaigrette, without making it too salty.

8 Moisten the squab and mushroom mixture with some of the vinaigrette, then add the parsley and toss gently. Put the leaves in another bowl, then toss them with a little of the vinaigrette.

9 Gently fold the mushroom and squab mixture into the leaves and distribute between 6 entrée plates. Tuck a leg in the centre of each salad, then drizzle any remaining vinaigrette around the edge of the salads and serve.

300g baby green beans, tops snapped off

sea salt

2 small heads garlic [preferably the purple variety]

extra virgin olive oil, for cooking

300g mixed mushrooms [such as Slippery Jack,
King Brown, shiitake or oyster], stalks trimmed

freshly ground white pepper

1 clove garlic, finely chopped

1–2 small, quite firm pears [such as Josephine or Corella]

125ml verjuice*

4–5 Aylesbury duck breasts, removed from the fridge
15 minutes before cooking

2 handfuls mesclun [see page xiii], washed and spin-dried

1 handful crisp leaves [such as baby cos lettuce hearts],
washed and spin-dried

1 bunch chives, finely chopped

Vinaigrette

60ml hazelnut oil

40ml extra virgin olive oil

20ml aged sherry vinegar

1 small eschalot, finely diced

Serves 6

Warm Salads of Grilled Duck Breast

This rich salad combines sautéed wild mushrooms or the beautiful King Brown mushrooms with roasted garlic cloves, and raw pear to provide freshness. A sherry vinegar-based vinaigrette using both hazelnut and extra virgin olive oil creates the perfect balance.

1 Preheat the oven to 160° C. Cook the beans in plenty of boiling salted water for 3 minutes or so, keeping them on the firm side, then drain and refresh under cold running water. Drain well.

2 Moisten the heads of garlic with extra virgin olive oil, then wrap in foil. Roast for 20–30 minutes [depending on the size] or until tender when pierced with a fine skewer. Remove the foil and allow to cool.

3 If using Slippery Jacks don't put them near water; rather use moistened paper towel to clean away any dirt. Cut the mushrooms into 1cm-thick slices.

4 Heat 20–40ml olive oil in a heavy-based frying pan over high heat until it just begins to smoke. Add the mushrooms, salt and pepper and sauté rapidly over medium heat until they have softened. Reduce the heat to low, then add the chopped garlic and sauté for another minute, then transfer to a covered plate.

5 To make the vinaigrette, whisk the oils, vinegar and eschalot to make a slightly acidic vinaigrette.

6 Separate the cooled garlic cloves, then remove the skins, aiming to keep the cloves as whole as possible.

7 Cut the pears into quarters lengthwise, slice off the cores neatly, then thinly slice lengthwise into a bowl containing the verjuice.

8 Carefully score the skin into the fat [but not the flesh] of each duck breast, making a neat diamond pattern; this enables the fat to be released as the breasts cook. Preheat a cast-iron or other heavy-based frying pan with a tiny amount of olive oil over high heat to near smoking temperature. Rub a little salt into the incisions of the duck skin, then cook skin-side down, reducing the temperature to low after 1 minute. Continue cooking for another 2 minutes or until the skin is crisp and golden, then flip over and cook until sealed. Rest, skin-side up, for 5 minutes on a plate; the flesh should be quite pink in the centre.

9 Toss the beans, mushrooms, salad leaves and drained pear with most of the vinaigrette and distribute between 6 flat entrée plates, along with the roasted garlic cloves.

10 Place the duck breasts skin-side down on a board and carve crosswise into 5mm-thick slices, then arrange on the plates. Garnish the salads with chives, finishing with a drizzle of the remaining vinaigrette.

300g Jerusalem artichokes, peeled and cut into 2cm dice	
2 litres water	
sea salt	
a good squeeze lemon juice	
2 cups flat-leaf parsley sprigs, washed and spin-dried	
½ bunch chives, finely chopped	
½ cup coriander leaves, washed and spin-dried, gently torn into small pieces	
20ml grapeseed oil	
24 large scallops	
freshly ground white pepper	

Vinaigrette

60ml hazelnut oil
40ml grapeseed oil
sea salt and freshly ground white pepper
2 teaspoons lime juice, or to taste

Serves 6

Warm Seared Scallop, Jerusalem Artichoke & Fresh Herb Salad

Scallops and Jerusalem artichokes really have an affinity, especially when laced with a little hazelnut oil vinaigrette. Combined with aromatic, savoury and spicy herbs this little salad makes an excellent entrée. If serving as a starter for a grand dinner, use half quantities.

1 Put the artichokes and cold salted water in a saucepan with the lemon juice, then bring to the boil and cook for 1–2 minutes. Drain and pat dry with paper towel.

2 Put the herbs in a bowl, then refrigerate until required.

3 To make the vinaigrette, whisk the ingredients to produce a tangy dressing; the hazelnut oil should be the predominant flavour.

4 Heat a heavy-based non-stick frying pan over high heat until very hot, then add half the grapeseed oil and briefly sauté the artichoke to gain a little colour. Place in a large warmed mixing bowl and cover to keep warm.

5 Rinse and dry the frying pan, then heat it over high heat with the remaining grapeseed oil to smoking point. Season the scallops with salt and pepper, then sear them for about 30 seconds on each side to gain a golden crust; this step is best done in 2 or 3 batches since the success depends on terrific heat in the pan.

6 As the scallops are cooked, transfer them to the bowl of artichokes, along with half the vinaigrette, and toss quickly. Add the herbs to the bowl of scallops and toss gently with your hands.

7 Distribute the salad between 6 flat entrée plates, then tuck the scallops and artichoke around the salad. Drizzle any remaining vinaigrette over each plate and serve immediately.

24 seedless green grapes, on the stem

250ml verjuice*

3 tablespoons rendered duck fat or extra virgin olive oil

3 Golden Delicious or 2 Granny Smith apples, peeled, cored and cut into eighths

1–2 tablespoons white sugar

a small slosh best quality cider vinegar*

400g cleaned duck livers, carefully checked and any greenish marks, fat and tubes removed

sea salt and freshly ground black pepper

40ml Calvados

3 handfuls mixed salad leaves [including wild rocket sprigs, small pieces of dandelion or radicchio, crisp baby cos hearts and spicy Asian greens such as tatsoi or mizuna], washed and spin-dried

4–6 red radishes, tops removed, thinly sliced

Vinaigrette

20–40ml best quality cider vinegar*

1 small clove garlic, any green shoot removed, smashed

1 heaped teaspoon Dijon mustard

1 small eschalot, very finely diced

40ml walnut oil

40ml extra virgin olive oil

20ml grapeseed oil

1 tablespoon rendered duck fat

sea salt and freshly ground black pepper

Serves 6

A Duck Liver Salad with Calvados, Glazed Apple & Grapes

Duck livers and apple are a delicious combination, particularly if the apple is slightly caramelised and spiked with a touch of cider vinegar. Calvados, the apple brandy from Normandy, has a complex fruit flavour that softens the richness of the duck livers in this salad. The apple may be cooked a little in advance but should not be cold, so transfer it to a warmed, covered plate and wrap in a heavy towel for up to one hour before serving.

1   Rinse the grapes on the stems under cold running water then detach from the stems. Bring the verjuice to the boil in a small saucepan and drop in the grapes. Remove the pan from the heat and allow the grapes to cool, then cut in halves lengthwise. [If seedless grapes are unavailable, this technique will make it easier to remove the seeds.]

2   To make the vinaigrette, put all the ingredients in a screw-top jar and shake well. Taste and correct the seasoning with salt and pepper and adjust the acidity with more vinegar, if desired; you are aiming for a fresh, rich flavour. Leave to stand, then discard the garlic after 15 minutes.

3   Heat 2 tablespoons of the duck fat in a large frying pan to very hot, then add the apple, scatter with sugar and toss to coat. Reduce the heat to medium and cook until slightly coloured, then turn over and cook for a minute longer. Add the vinegar and toss quickly, then turn onto a warmed plate and cover to keep warm.

4   This next step will be easier if done in a small pan in 2 batches. Heat the remaining duck fat until very hot but not smoking. Season the livers lightly with salt and pepper and sear to colour them on both sides; they should feel slightly springy to the fingertip and still be pink in the centre. Add the Calvados and toss quickly, then transfer the livers to a wide bowl. Reduce the juices to a syrupy consistency over high heat and pour over the livers, then toss gently. [The Calvados may ignite if you are cooking with gas so take care.]

5   Put the leaves and radishes in a wide salad bowl, moisten with the vinaigrette and toss using your hands. Distribute the salad, apple and grapes between 6 entrée plates. Slice each liver into 2–3 pieces, moisten with a touch of vinaigrette and divide between the salads. Serve immediately.

2 carrots [about 400g], cut into very fine julienne

3 teaspoons sea salt

a few white peppercorns, cracked

½ teaspoon white sugar

40ml tarragon vinegar or white-wine vinegar

6 sets lambs' brains,* peeled

6 kipfler potatoes, cut into 3mm-thick slices

extra virgin olive oil

freshly ground white pepper

6 small radishes, tops removed, cut into 2mm-thick slices

3 handfuls small green leaves [including tiny sprigs rocket and watercress, mizuna, sliced witlof, 5 torn mint leaves and purslane if available], washed and spin-dried

Court-bouillon

750ml cold water

250ml dry white wine

1 onion, sliced

1 carrot, scrubbed and sliced

1 stalk celery, white part only, sliced

3 small mushrooms, sliced

bouquet garni* [thyme, bay leaf and parsley stalks, all wrapped in a muslin cloth tied with kitchen twine]

sea salt and freshly ground white pepper

Sauce ravigote

½ teaspoon Dijon mustard

80ml extra virgin olive oil

20ml tarragon vinegar

2 teaspoons small salted capers, soaked in warm water, rinsed and dried

1 tablespoon snipped French tarragon

1 tablespoon snipped chervil

1 tablespoon snipped chives

2 spring onions, white part only, trimmed and finely sliced

2–3 cornichons,* roughly chopped

sea salt and freshly ground white pepper

Serves 6

Lambs' Brain Salad Ravigote

Brains are delicate and delicious morsels, more commonly served deep-fried with their texture protected by a coating of breadcrumb; this delivers crunch that contrasts with their silken texture. Here the complexity and added acidic ingredients offer another level of contrast to the texture of the brains. The French have a wonderfully rich dish from Grenoble where poached brains are bathed in burnt butter with capers, parsley and crunchy little croûtons. The ideal sauce for a salad of poached brains is the classic ravigote, which is really a vinaigrette flavoured with cornichons,* spring onion, capers and fines herbes.* You will need to start making the lightly pickled carrot mixture the night before you wish to serve this salad.

This salad would sit comfortably followed by grilled whole snapper simply drizzled with a little extra virgin olive oil and lemon juice. Dessert might consist of sliced pears in a bowl of ice and a mature goat's cheese with toasted walnut bread.

1   The night before serving the salad, season the carrot with the salt, peppercorns, sugar and vinegar [a little more may be needed depending on the sweetness of the carrot], then stir to combine. Cover with plastic film and refrigerate.

2   On the day of serving, bring the court-bouillon ingredients slowly to the boil, skim and simmer for 20 minutes. Strain through a fine sieve, then adjust the seasoning so it is on the slightly salty side.

3   Poach the peeled brains in the court-bouillon very gently over low heat for 6–8 minutes or until they feel firm to the fingertip. Using a slotted spoon, transfer them to a wide bowl and pour over enough court-bouillon to cover them, then leave for 1 hour to cool. Drain well before carving each half-set into 3–4 slices. Cover with plastic film.

4   Meanwhile, steam the potato over a saucepan of boiling water for 12–14 minutes, then transfer to a plate, drizzle with oil and lightly season with salt and pepper.

5   To make the sauce ravigote, combine the ingredients in a bowl and whisk gently. Adjust the seasoning to taste.

6   Scatter the potato over 6 entrée plates. Assemble the radish and leaves in a bowl. Moisten with 20ml of the sauce ravigote and fold gently with your hands, then scatter over the potato, leaving a space in the centre.

7   Using tongs, place a bed of carrot in the centre of each plate. Use a flat spatula or wide knife to place the slices of brain on top, then coat the brains with the remaining sauce ravigote. Serve immediately.

2 small heads garlic	sea salt and freshly ground black pepper
extra virgin olive oil	60ml extra virgin olive oil
3 × 2cm-thick slices day-old sourdough bread, crusts removed	150g skinless thinly sliced smoked speck [ask the butcher or delicatessen to slice this for you]
aged red-wine vinegar [such as Forum Cabernet vinegar* or Banyuls*], for drizzling	250–300g unsprayed tender young dandelion leaves [about 1 bunch], well washed and spin-dried
4 eggs, at fridge temperature	**Serves 6**
1 teaspoon Dijon mustard	

Warm Salad of Dandelion, Crisp Smoked Speck & Roasted Garlic

The bitterness of the dandelion leaves is offset by the soft, oily garlic cloves and chopped hard-boiled egg. The crisp, smoky tang of the speck adds saltiness, while the vinegar-spiked bread provides much-needed acidity. You will need to work quickly at the last minute to keep the ingredients hot since the dressing includes the rendered fat from the speck. Don't be concerned if the garlic breaks up when it is peeled; this is intentional. Serve this rustic salad all year round as an entrée to stimulate the palate before a baked snapper, accompanied by a fresh-herb mayonnaise and steamed waxy potatoes.

1 Preheat the oven to 160°C. Check the heads of garlic are clean and firm, then rub lightly with olive oil and wrap in foil. Bake for 30–40 minutes or until tender, checking after 20 minutes by piercing with a fine skewer.

2 Meanwhile, tear the bread into rough chunks directly into a wide mixing bowl, then splash the pieces with enough vinegar to dampen well.

3 Meanwhile, prick the eggs with a fine pin and gently lower them into a saucepan of boiling water. Return to the boil, then retrieve one egg after 3 minutes and set aside for the vinaigrette, leaving the others to cook for a further 7 minutes. Refresh the 10-minute eggs under cold running water, then shell them and coarsely chop.

4 To make the vinaigrette, crack the 3-minute egg over a small bowl then scoop the egg out into the bowl. Mash with a fork, work in the mustard and a tiny pinch of salt then whisk in the oil. Add some pepper and set aside.

5 Preheat an overhead griller to medium. Meanwhile, separate the roasted garlic cloves, discarding the skin and transferring the cloves to a small bowl. Cover with plastic film.

6 Lay the speck on a cake-cooling rack sitting over a shallow baking tray so that the fat can drain off as it cooks. Grill the speck, watching it closely so that neither the speck nor the rendered fat burns; the speck should be crisp. Remove from the griller and leave the fat in the baking tray.

7 Put a salad bowl and 6 deep entrée plates into the warm oven; the oven door might need to stay open for a few minutes if it is too hot.

8 This is where time is of the essence. Heat a good-sized frying pan or stock pot that will hold the dandelion leaves and add 2 tablespoons of the rendered speck fat. Sauté the dandelion in the fat until it softens, season lightly [keeping the saltiness of the speck in mind], then turn into the warm salad bowl. Add the bread, chopped egg and garlic, then add the vinaigrette and toss well. Crumble the speck with your hands and scatter over the salad, then serve immediately.

18–24 baby beetroot, with 2cm stalk attached, scrubbed

5 fresh figs [preferably the Honey variety]

2 handfuls [or whatever is available] small beetroot leaves, washed and spin-dried

3 handfuls small frisée lettuce leaves, washed and spin-dried

1 handful small rocket or watercress sprigs, washed and spin-dried

2 tablespoons lemon thyme leaves

Goat's cheese fritters

500g fresh goat's cheese [in log form]

plain flour, seasoned with salt and pepper for dusting

2 eggs, lightly beaten with ¼ teaspoon salt

3 cups dried breadcrumbs [Japanese panko crumbs give a light crunchy crust]

1.5–2 litres peanut oil, for deep-frying

Vinaigrette

1 small clove garlic, any green shoot removed, finely chopped

1 eschalot, finely chopped

1 teaspoon Dijon mustard

60ml extra virgin olive oil

2–3 teaspoons aged red-wine vinegar [such as Forum Cabernet vinegar*]

sea salt and freshly ground white pepper

Serves 6 as a light lunch

Salad of Fresh Goat's Cheese Fritters, Baby Beetroot & Figs

This is a variation on a salad we served at Bistro Moncur many years ago – sadly none of us can remember the precise ingredients [and so much the better in many ways]. Originally we used a very fresh, lovely cheese that was presented as a sample by a wonderfully honest farmer who knocked on the back door of the restaurant one day. He formed the cheese into cylinders so that all we had to do was slice off discs, then crumb and fry them to order. Like many pure and original products, this cheese is no longer available so I now use a matured goat's cheese such as the delicious Holy Goat Mature Skyla brand. The crust should be sliced off before the slices are crumbed. To ensure that the fritters don't collapse completely when deep-frying, look for a firm log of goat's cheese, but not the hard matured type since this will take away from the freshness of this salad.

1 Preheat the oven to 160°C. Wrap the beetroot individually in foil, then bake for 30 minutes or until they are tender when pierced with a fine skewer. Unwrap the beetroot, then peel and remove the stalks. Cut any larger bulbs in half. Cover and set aside.

2 To make the goat's cheese fritters, slice the goat's cheese into 1cm–wide discs; there should be at least 12 pieces. Dust the cheese with the seasoned flour, then pass through the beaten egg and then the breadcrumbs. Lay the fritters on a baking tray lined with baking paper and refrigerate until ready to fry; don't crumb the cheese more than 2 hours ahead as the crumbs will soften.

3 To make the vinaigrette, whisk together all the ingredients, then taste and adjust the seasoning.

4 When you are ready to serve, cut the figs in half lengthwise to display their pretty interiors.

5 Heat the oil in a large deep saucepan until it registers 180°C on a candy thermometer.✳

6 Meanwhile, quickly moisten the beetroot with half the vinaigrette and, in a separate bowl, the salad and thyme leaves with the remainder. Assemble the beetroot and leaves on 6 flat entrée plates, then top with 3 quartered figs per serve, cut-side up.

7 Fry the fritters in batches until crisp and pale golden, draining them on paper towel as they are cooked. Tuck them into the salads against the beetroot to give the salad some height. Serve immediately.

Winter Salads

Salades d'hiver

60g walnut kernels

350g Brussels sprouts, outer leaves discarded

3 handfuls small watercress sprigs, washed and spin-dried

4 pale inner stalks celery, including the leaves

40ml lemon juice

1½ crisp eating apples, washed and cored

1 quantity Alex Herbert's Roquefort Dressing [see page 176]

50g Roquefort, crumbled

Serves 6

Brussels Sprout Leaf, Watercress & Celery Salad with Roquefort Dressing

This is a salad to make in early winter when the new-season Brussels sprouts are sweet. Choose small ones, which should have very little aroma other than a grassy quality; this indicates real freshness, which is essential when using the raw leaves. The watercress offers a touch of spice while the crisp celery contributes a fresh bite of flavour and texture to the palate. The salty acidity of Roquefort is enhanced by the nuttiness of toasted ground walnuts. Follow with a slow-roasted pork neck that has been larded with slivers of garlic and lemon thyme. A purée of one-third boiled fennel and two-thirds steamed potatoes scented with ground star anise makes a good garnish, along with some green peas. Perhaps an old-fashioned lemon delicious pudding would be the right dessert for this winter menu.

1 Preheat the oven to 150°C. Lightly toast the walnuts in the oven for 5–10 minutes, then leave to cool and coarsely chop.

2 Slice 5mm off the base of each Brussels sprout, gently pull away the leaves, wash and spin-dry them, then add to a bowl with the watercress.

3 Cut off the celery leaves, then separate them. Cut the celery into 3cm-long matchsticks. Add both to the bowl of salad leaves.

4 Put the lemon juice in a bowl. Thinly slice the apples, then toss with the lemon juice and drain.

5 Add the apple to the salad bowl, then moisten with three-quarters of the dressing and toss gently with your hands. Distribute the crumbled Roquefort evenly over the salad and drizzle with vinaigrette, dust with the chopped walnuts and serve at once. Alternatively, divide the salad between 6 deep entrée plates.

12 Jerusalem artichokes [the size of an egg], scrubbed under running water, then dried

extra virgin olive oil, for cooking

sea salt and freshly ground white pepper

4 eggs, at fridge temperature

2 handfuls small watercress sprigs, washed and spin-dried

1 head white witlof [use only 3–4cm of the tips]

1 head red witlof [use only 3–4cm of the tips]

4–5 mint leaves, torn into little pieces

1 × 120g jar salmon roe or ocean trout roe

Crème fraîche and chive dressing

1 bunch chives, finely chopped

80ml crème fraîche*

20ml grapeseed oil

2 teaspoons lemon juice

sea salt and freshly ground white pepper

a little cold water or verjuice* [optional], to thin the dressing

Serves 6 as a starter

Roast Jerusalem Artichokes, Witlof & Salmon Roe Salad with Crème Fraîche & Chive Dressing

Knobbly Jerusalem artichoke tubers look a lot like root ginger. They have a thin skin, crisp texture when eaten raw and are soft when cooked; I especially love them roasted. They make a delicious soup and marry so well with seared scallops [see Warm Seared Scallop, Jerusalem Artichoke & Fresh Herb Salad on page 159] but are somewhat indigestible and can cause flatulence. This salad is adapted from a starter dish I served when I owned Claude's Restaurant in Sydney. The artichokes were originally roasted, then the tops were split open and filled with crème fraîche* and chives and topped with salmon roe – a perfect winter starter for a four-course menu. In this version, watercress, witlof tips, a touch of mint and sliced hard-boiled eggs are moistened with a chive and cream dressing to complement the earthy flavour of the artichokes. The salmon roe is scattered over the salad, giving a big burst of flavour. If salmon roe is not to your liking, substitute thinly sliced anchovies.

1 Preheat the oven 180°C. Cut a thin slice from one end of each artichoke so that it will stand upright on a baking tray. Paint lightly with olive oil, then season with salt and pepper. Bake the artichokes for 20–30 minutes or until tender when pierced with a fine skewer. Remove and break into quarters with your hands while still warm, then leave to cool to room temperature.

2 Prick the eggs with a pin then boil them for 10 minutes. Drain and refresh under cold running water. Shell the eggs, then cut using an egg slicer [they may also be roughly chopped].

3 To make the dressing, combine the chives, crème fraîche, grapeseed oil and lemon juice in a small bowl and season with salt and pepper to taste. The lemon juice may cause the dressing to thicken so dilute to a runny consistency with water or verjuice if necessary.

4 Moisten the artichokes, watercress, witlof and mint with some dressing, then add the chopped egg. Toss gently with your hands, then divide between 6 flat entrée plates. Drop a few salmon roe here and there over the salads and drizzle over any remaining dressing, then serve.

450g peeled and seeded pumpkin, cut into small dice

extra virgin olive oil, for cooking

sea salt and freshly ground black pepper

350g Jerusalem artichokes, peeled and cut into 3mm-thick slices

1 teaspoon powdered asafoetida [optional]

8–10 large Sicilian green olives, flesh pared from the stones

1 tablespoon thyme leaves

2 cups finely shaved radicchio

120–150g mature goat's cheese, rind removed

Vinaigrette

75ml extra virgin olive oil

finely grated zest of 1 lemon

20ml aged balsamic vinegar

sea salt and freshly ground black pepper

Serves 6

Salad of Pumpkin, Jerusalem Artichoke, Green Olives & Mature Goat's Cheese

Jerusalem artichokes are not actually artichokes but rather the roots of a North American relative of the sunflower plant. They are a winter vegetable with a delicious nutty flavour. Jerusalem artichokes make a splendid soup, and may be added to a potato purée, boiled as a vegetable and even eaten raw. However, many find them hard to digest and they can cause flatulence. When cooking Jerusalem artichokes, I recommend adding 1 teaspoon powdered asafoetida for every 500ml of water, then boiling them until tender to make them more digestible. Asafoetida is available from Herbie's Spices® in Rozelle, New South Wales, and via mail order: herbies.com.au.

Here, the exciting melange of flavours and textures is contrasted with shaved radicchio to offer a touch of bitterness.

1 Preheat the oven to 110°C. Toss the pumpkin with 20ml or so extra virgin olive oil and a little salt and pepper, then roast for 15 minutes or until tender, tossing occasionally to colour evenly. Remove from the oven and cover loosely with foil to retain the heat.

2 Meanwhile, blanch the artichoke in boiling water [add the asafoetida if desired] for 2 minutes, checking after 1 minute since it should still retain a slight crunch. Drain well, pat dry with paper towel, then transfer to a large mixing bowl with the olives and thyme leaves.

3 To make the vinaigrette, place the olive oil, lemon zest and balsamic vinegar in a screw-top jar, then shake. Season with salt and pepper to taste; it should have a fresh, complex flavour.

4 Add the warm pumpkin and radicchio to the artichokes and olives, then moisten with most of the vinaigrette. Fold the ingredients together using your hands, then divide among 6 entrée plates.

5 Use a sharp knife to shave the goat's cheese and scatter it over the salads, then moisten with more dressing.

120g Puy-style lentils

2 cloves garlic, any green shoot removed, 1 lightly smashed and 1 whole

120ml extra virgin olive oil

1 bunch curly-leaf parsley, leaves picked, washed and thoroughly dried and 8 stalks reserved

sea salt and freshly ground black pepper

20ml walnut oil or hazelnut oil

30ml aged sherry vinegar, or to taste

1 small head celeriac, peeled and cut into fine matchsticks

400g button mushrooms, stalks removed, caps thinly sliced

finely grated zest of 1 lemon

1 lemon

180g fresh goat's cheese, crumbled into small pieces

6 sage leaves, torn into small pieces

Serves 6

Winter Salad of Lentils, Celeriac, Mushrooms & Fresh Goat's Cheese with Parsley Vinaigrette

This substantial salad suits being served during the cooler months as an entrée or main course followed by a cheese such as Roquefort and a simple leaf salad for a light lunch. The gentle, earthy flavours contrast with the acidity of the goat's cheese and the freshness of the sage.

1 Discard any small stones from the lentils and rinse with cold water. Place the lentils in a saucepan with the smashed garlic, 20ml of the olive oil and the parsley stalks tied with a piece of kitchen twine. Add a little salt and simmer over low heat for 20 minutes or more until tender, tasting and adjusting the salt level after 15 minutes. Drain, discarding the garlic and parsley stalks.

2 Meanwhile, set aside one-third of the parsley leaves to be finely chopped. Bring a saucepan of salted water to the boil with the whole garlic clove and simmer for a few minutes, then add the remaining parsley leaves. Boil for 5 minutes or until the leaves are very soft indeed. Drain, discard the garlic and refresh the parsley in a sieve under cold running water. Drain again and squeeze out some of the water. Place the blanched parsley in a blender, then add a little salt and pepper, the remaining olive oil, the nut oil and 20ml of the vinegar. Blend until smooth, then adjust the acidity with more vinegar to a sharp finish and correct the seasoning.

3 Moisten the warm lentils with some of the parsley vinaigrette. Add the celeriac, mushroom and grated lemon zest, then moisten with more vinaigrette and toss gently.

4 Slice the tips off the lemon so that it sits firmly on a chopping board. Using a sharp paring knife and holding the lemon with the other hand, run the knife close to the flesh and remove the skin and pith following the contour of the fruit. Holding the lemon over a bowl with one hand, slice between each fillet to extract them. Dice the flesh into small pieces, discarding the seeds. Mix the lemon pieces with the lentil and celeriac mixture.

5 Finely chop the remaining parsley. Distribute the salad between 6 deep entrée plates, then scatter with the goat's cheese, sage and parsley.

150g walnut kernels	
50g Demerara caster sugar	
40ml verjuice*	
1 small handful pale celery leaves	
1 stalk celery, finely sliced on the diagonal	
2 heads witlof, leaves separated	
100g watercress, leaves picked	
1 head radicchio, washed and spin-dried, leaves separated and torn	
80g Roquefort, at room temperature, crumbled	

Alex Herbert's Roquefort dressing

20g Roquefort
80ml crème fraîche*
30ml lemon juice, or to taste
sea salt and freshly ground black pepper

Serves 4–6

Alex Herbert's Roquefort Salad

Alex Herbert and her partner, Howard, own a wonderful restaurant called Bird Cow Fish in Surry Hills, Sydney. Alex has worked with some remarkable chefs including Maggie Beer. The fare at Bird Cow Fish has Alex's unique stamp of superbly fresh seasonal produce cooked with passion. Here is a delicious salad as written by Alex, a much-respected colleague with a fine palate.

1   Toast the walnuts in a frying pan over low heat until dry, then sprinkle with Demerara caster sugar; the sugar will melt and caramelise. Once the sugar has reached a rich dark brown, deglaze the pan with a generous splash of verjuice; the verjuice should evaporate completely. Set aside.

2   To make the dressing, in a small bowl, mix the Roquefort with the crème fraîche and add lemon juice to taste. Whisk to achieve a good balance between the acidity of the crème fraîche and the lemon juice and the richness of the cheese, as well as to make a dressing that is not too thick. Season with salt and pepper and adjust if necessary.

3   Assemble the celery leaves, celery, witlof, watercress, walnuts, radicchio and Roquefort in a bowl. Pour over the dressing, toss and serve.

12 small onions, unpeeled, pierced through the centre with a sharp paring knife

coarse salt or rock salt, for cooking

150g Puy-style lentils

1 clove garlic, skin on, lightly bruised

100ml extra virgin olive oil, plus extra for cooking

1 bay leaf

a few sprigs thyme

1 strip scrubbed lemon zest

sea salt and freshly ground black pepper

5 radicchio leaves, washed and spin-dried, roughly shredded

400g cherry tomatoes, washed and halved

20ml good-quality aged red-wine vinegar [such as Forum Cabernet vinegar*]

100g Pecorino Romano, finely shaved

Serves 6

Salad of Roast Onion, Lentils, Cherry Tomatoes & Radicchio

Lentils are a fine source of protein and have a delicate nutty flavour that works well with the sweetness of roast onions. The tomatoes contribute acidity, while radicchio offers some bitterness to balance the dish. A salad for any time, particularly the cooler months.

1 Preheat the oven to 180°C. Place the onions on a bed of coarse salt and roast for 30–40 minutes or until they are soft when pierced with a fine skewer. Remove from oven, peel while still warm, then discard the skins.

2 Meanwhile, remove any small stones from the lentils and rinse with cold water. Place in a saucepan, cover well with water, then add the garlic, 20ml of the olive oil, bay leaf, thyme and lemon zest. Bring to the boil, add a pinch of salt and simmer over low heat for 30 minutes or until tender; this may vary so check after 20 minutes. The lentils should offer very little resistance. Drain, discard the herbs, garlic and lemon zest, then adjust the seasoning to taste with salt and pepper. Leave to cool, then stir in three-quarters of the radicchio.

3 Lay the tomato in a colander, sprinkle with salt and leave for 20–30 minutes, then pat dry with paper towel. Place in a shallow, wide frying pan with a slosh of extra virgin olive oil and some pepper and warm very gently over low heat for 5 minutes to soften them. Under no circumstances take an eye off them; don't allow the heat to increase beyond blood temperature. Remove from the heat when done.

4 Carefully break the onions into 2 or 3 pieces each, without fussing too much. Distribute the lentils between 6 deep entrée plates, then arrange the onion here and there on the top, along with the tomato.

5 Whisk the remaining 80ml olive oil with the vinegar and season to taste, then use to moisten the vegetables. Scatter with the remaining radicchio and shaved pecorino and serve.

½ radicchio, washed and spin-dried, roughly shredded

½ witlof, roughly shredded

1 handful sorrel, stalks removed, washed just before roughly shredding

4 red radishes, tops removed, thinly sliced

½ head baby fennel, cut into matchsticks

1 handful mint, roughly torn

1 handful flat-leaf parsley leaves, washed and dried

1 Lebanese cucumber, cut into matchsticks

1 salad onion, cut into matchsticks

1 Jalapeno chilli, seeded and finely sliced

120g sopressa, cut into matchsticks

½ cup dried cooked or drained tinned chick peas, skins removed

2 vine-ripened tomatoes, each cut into 6–8 wedges

60g Gruyère, grated

Dressing

extra virgin olive oil, for drizzling

lemon juice, to taste

sea salt and freshly ground black pepper

Serves 4

House Chopped Salad

While contributing to a masterclass for the Melbourne Food and Wine Festival in 2008, I enjoyed this wonderful salad at Neil Perry's splendid Rockpool Bar & Grill Melbourne. Neil has kindly contributed the recipe for his salad. He recommends that it be chopped just before serving, which might sound a bit daunting but, believe me, the result is really worth the effort. Make sure all the ingredients are as fresh as possible. Sopressa is available in delicatessens.

1   Simply toss all the salad ingredients together and dress with extra virgin olive oil and lemon juice, then season with salt and pepper to taste.

2 cloves garlic, thinly sliced

6 sprigs thyme

1 large bay leaf, broken into small pieces

1 tablespoon cracked black peppercorns

5–6 tablespoons sea salt flakes

6 duck legs, rinsed and thoroughly dried

700ml – 1 litre olive oil [a quarter being extra virgin]

Braised lentils

120g Puy-style lentils

about 300ml light chicken stock

1 small onion, finely diced

½ small carrot, peeled and finely diced

1 bay leaf

sea salt and freshly ground black pepper

20ml extra virgin olive oil

Salad

100g walnut kernels, roughly broken into quarters

20ml walnut oil

1 baby cos lettuce, outer leaves discarded, inner leaves washed and spin-dried

1–2 small heads witlof, damaged outer leaves discarded

a few radicchio leaves, washed and spin-dried, torn into small pieces

1 large handful small rocket or watercress sprigs, washed and spin-dried

Vinaigrette

1 clove garlic, smashed

40ml extra virgin olive oil

40ml grapeseed oil

20ml walnut oil

20–30ml best quality cider vinegar* or aged sherry vinegar

sea salt and freshly ground white pepper

Serves 6

Confit Duck Leg Salad with Lentils & Fried Walnuts

This is a good entrée for a winter lunch followed by grilled fish dressed with sauce vierge.* The confit and lentils may be cooked the day before, leaving very little work to finish the salad at the last minute. The salty sweetness of the warm duck legs complements the earthy flavour of the lentils, nuttiness of the walnuts and freshness of the leaves.

If time is an issue, you can purchase splendid ready-made confit duck legs prepared in the traditional manner, for example the Barossa range of products.

1 The day before, select a non-reactive dish that will accommodate the duck in one layer. Scatter the base with half the garlic, herbs, peppercorns and salt. Place the duck legs on top, then scatter with the remaining garlic, herbs, peppercorns and salt. Cover and refrigerate for 3–4 hours.

2 Remove the duck legs from the salt mixture, rinse under cold running water and dry thoroughly with paper towel.

3 In a large, heavy-based saucepan, heat the oil until it registers 80°C on a candy thermometer,* then add the duck legs. Cook between 70 and 80°C for 1 hour or until the meat begins to come away from the bone. Pierce a leg to be sure the juices are clear and not pink. Transfer the confit duck legs to a plate to cool thoroughly before refrigerating them. Retain the cooking oil.

4 To make the braised lentils, remove any small stones from the lentils then rinse with cold water. Combine the lentils, stock, onion, carrot and bay leaf in a saucepan, then bring to the boil and season lightly with salt and pepper. Simmer over low heat for 20 minutes or until the lentils are just tender and not disintegrating. Drain and discard the bay leaf, then add the olive oil and season to taste.

5 To prepare the salad, preheat the oven to 190°C. Lightly grease an ovenproof frying pan with a little of the reserved confit oil, then roast the duck legs, skinless-side up first for a few minutes then turn over and cook until they are nicely coloured.

6 To make the vinaigrette, rub a small bowl with the smashed garlic and discard the debris. Whisk together the remaining ingredients and adjust the seasoning.

7 Toss the walnuts in walnut oil. Heat the oil in a frying pan over high heat until fairly hot then reduce the temperature and fry the walnuts. Keep an eye on them since they can burn rather quickly. Drain immediately in a sieve.

8 To serve the salad, lay some cos leaves on a platter. Coarsely tear the remainder, then add the witlof, radicchio and rocket and dress with most of the vinaigrette. Transfer the leaves, lentils, duck legs and walnuts to the platter and moisten the duck legs with the remaining vinaigrette. Serve at once.

1.2kg duck giblets, uncleaned [to yield 600g cleaned]	

¼ cup sea salt flakes
1 tablespoon black peppercorns, cracked
1 bay leaf, broken into small pieces
4 sprigs thyme
1 clove garlic, sliced
400–500g rendered duck fat
2 heads garlic
olive oil, for cooking
75g walnut kernels, broken into small pieces
2 teaspoons grapeseed oil
3–4 handfuls mixed salad leaves [including radicchio or dandelion, witlof tips, frisée lettuce and small sprigs of rocket and watercress], washed and spin-dried [except the witlof]
4–5 red radishes, tops removed, thinly sliced

Duck skin crackling

2 duck necks
20ml water
1 small bay leaf

Vinaigrette

1 clove garlic, smashed
60ml walnut oil
20ml grapeseed oil
2 teaspoons aged red-wine vinegar [such as Forum Cabernet vinegar*] or aged sherry vinegar
sea salt and freshly ground black pepper

Serves 6 as an entrée

Salad of Confit Duck Giblets & Duck Skin Crackling

Stephanie Alexander has been a major influence on my cooking. Our friendship began when I dined at her first humble North Fitzroy establishment in the mid-1970s, where her cooking transformed the Melbourne restaurant scene. Stephanie's interpretation of authentic French cuisine and the occasional Italian dish were a revelation to a dining public used to the grandeur of the city's long-established restaurants. Stephanie moved her restaurant to a grand mansion in Hawthorn, where the fare expanded the French classic repertoire with exciting dishes from the Nouvelle Cuisine revolution of that time. Stephanie's menu often included delicious dishes from the tradition of French bourgeois cuisine and here is a dish inspired by one I remember enjoying in the late 1980s. Here is how Stephanie and I remember this dish.

The technique known as confit originated as a means of preserving the product from a harvest of pigs and poultry at its peak in order to enjoy it over the following months, as well as to make sure every part of the flesh was used. Duck giblets are especially delicious when prepared in this manner since this method transforms the natural offal taste into a rich but subtle flavour with a robust palate of continuing length. The duck crackling offers a contrast of texture to the salad leaves spiked with fried walnuts and roasted garlic. This is a delicious entrée for a winter menu that might be followed by a simple roast chicken or game bird.

1 Remove the skin from the giblets with a very sharp knife. Lay 1 giblet at a time on a chopping board, then insert the knife tip between the skin and the flesh. Hold the giblet against the board, then slide the knife around it to detach the skin; this may take a few attempts before you get the knack. Your butcher should be able to do this for you. Be sure that all the skin is removed.

2 Put the giblets in a non-reactive dish large enough to accommodate them in one layer, then scatter with the salt, cracked pepper, bay leaf, thyme and garlic. Toss so the giblets are lightly coated with the salt mixture, then cover with plastic film and refrigerate for 4–5 hours.

3 Use moistened paper towel to remove all the salt mixture from the giblets, then dry them thoroughly with more paper towel.

4 Heat the duck fat in a heavy-based saucepan until it registers 80°C on a candy thermometer,* then add the giblets. Regulate the temperature to between 70 and 80°C and cook the giblets for about 1½ hours or until they are tender when pierced with a fine skewer. Transfer to a bowl to cool.

5 Preheat the oven to 160°C. Moisten the heads of garlic with olive oil and wrap in foil, then bake for 30–40 minutes or until they are tender when pierced with a fine skewer. Leave them to cool for 5 minutes, then carefully separate and peel each clove.

6   Toss the walnuts in the grapeseed oil and spread on a baking tray, then toast in the oven until lightly coloured. Keep an eye on them since they can burn rather quickly.

7   Meanwhile, for the duck skin crackling, ease the skin away from the thick ends of the duck necks, then slowly slide off the skin. The skin should now be inside out and have a small amount of fat and a tube still attached; discard these. Cut the skin into 15mm ribbons and put in the fridge. The necks can be roasted and used in a stock, if desired.

8   Place the ribbons of duck skin in a small frying pan with the water and the bay leaf and cook over low–medium heat until the skin is crisp and the fat looks clear. The fat will spit a bit so take care.

9   Drain the duck crackling on paper towel and keep it warm in the turned-off oven with the door slightly ajar. Drain the fat from the giblets and put them in the oven to warm a little.

10 To make the vinaigrette, combine all the ingredients.

11 Assemble the leaves, roasted garlic, walnuts and radish in a large mixing bowl, then moisten with enough vinaigrette to coat them lightly and toss with your hands.

12 Distribute the leaves and radishes between 6 deep entrée plates. Thinly slice the giblets and moisten with vinaigrette, then share between the salads, finishing with the crackling. Serve immediately.

125ml dry white wine	3–4 pale inner stalks celery [including leaves], washed and shaved into 3mm-thick slices, leaves torn
1.2 litres cold water	juice of ½ lemon
60ml extra virgin olive oil	100g Roquefort or Saint Agur blue cheese, crumbled
1 clove garlic, unpeeled and sliced, any green shoot removed	50g walnut kernels, chopped
½ small carrot, sliced	a few drops walnut oil
1 small onion, sliced	**Vinaigrette**
1 bay leaf	40ml walnut oil
4–5 sprigs thyme	20ml grapeseed oil
a few black peppercorns, cracked	20ml crème fraîche*
2 strips scrubbed orange zest	sea salt and freshly ground white pepper
3 teaspoons sea salt, or to taste	**Serves 6 as an accompaniment**
6 large witlof, damaged outer leaves discarded, cut in half lengthwise	

Salad of Cooked Witlof, Shaved Celery & Roquefort

Here is a lovely salad to accompany garlic and rosemary-scented roast veal [see opposite], sauced with a *déglaçage** of white wine and reduced veal stock. The slight bitterness of the witlof softens as it cooks with the celery, offering a firmer texture and fresh flavour to the dish. The salty Roquefort and unusual vinaigrette make this a very interesting dish. I recommend assembling the salad one hour before serving to allow the flavours to develop. This salad is best served very cold.

1 Preheat the oven to 150°C. Bring the wine, water, olive oil, garlic, carrot, onion, bay leaf, thyme, peppercorns, orange zest and salt slowly to the boil in a large saucepan over low heat and simmer for 15 minutes, then strain. Meanwhile, assemble the witlof in one layer in a suitably sized deep stainless-steel roasting pan or ceramic baking dish, cover with the strained cooking liquor, then cover the surface with baking paper and seal with foil. Bake for 30 minutes or until the witlof are tender but still hold their shape. Remove from the oven and cool the witlof in the liquor completely before refrigerating.

2 Assemble the salad about 1 hour before serving. Remove the witlof from the liquor and place 2 halves each on 6 entree plates. Toss the shaved celery in the lemon juice, then drain. Scatter the celery and celery leaves over the witlof.

3 To make the vinaigrette, whisk the ingredients well and adjust the seasoning with salt and pepper, then pour over the salads. Scatter with Roquefort, then cover with plastic film and return to the fridge for 1 hour.

4 Toss the walnuts with the walnut oil, then toss in a dry frying pan over medium heat. Keep an eye on them since they burn rather quickly. Add the warm walnuts to the chilled salads at the last minute, then serve.

1.2kg aged beef oyster blade, fat trimmed

6 cloves garlic, any green shoot removed, cut into thin slivers

sea salt and freshly ground black pepper

extra virgin olive oil, for cooking

60ml Armagnac* or cognac

1 piece pork skin from the back of the loin with a 1cm layer of fat still attached [large enough to wrap around the beef]

1 large bunch thyme

3 bay leaves

4 strips scrubbed orange zest, finely chopped

350g young thin carrots [not baby ones], peeled

1 × 750ml bottle pinot noir or Côtes du Rhône

Salad

2 handfuls dandelion leaves, torn into small pieces, washed and spin-dried

3 handfuls mesclun [see page xiii], washed and spin-dried

6 cornichons,* sliced lengthwise into slivers

4–5 truss tomatoes, cut into 15mm pieces

2 tablespoons thyme leaves, lightly chopped

⅓ cup finely shredded flat-leaf parsley

Vinaigrette

100ml extra virgin olive oil

40ml reserved cooking liquor

20ml Banyuls,* or to taste

sea salt and freshly ground black pepper

Serves 6 as a starter

Salad of Slow-cooked Beef with Bitter & Savoury Greens

The culinary term *daube* refers to flavoursome cuts of beef such as cheek or oyster blade cooked very slowly with herbs, pork skin and a good red wine, all of which add flavour and body to the sauce. Use a heavy-based casserole that accommodates the meat snugly. Serve as a starter before a fish-based main course or double the recipe and serve as a principal dish with a substantial dessert to follow.

1 Preheat the oven to 120°C. Make tiny incisions all over the oyster blade, then insert the garlic. Dry the meat with paper towel and season with salt, pepper and olive oil. Heat 20ml olive oil in a flameproof casserole with a lid and brown the meat on all sides. Add the Armagnac and warm a little, then ignite with a match. Shake the pan until the flames extinguish. Transfer the meat to a plate, strain and reserve the juices then wash and dry the casserole.

2 Lay the piece of pork skin on a bench top and scatter with the thyme, bay leaves and orange zest. Lay the oyster blade on top and roll up to enclose. Tie with kitchen twine at 2cm intervals.

3 Transfer the beef to the casserole with the carrots and wine and bring to the boil; the meat must be submerged so a little more wine may be required. Skim to remove any foam, then taste and adjust the seasoning. Add the reserved beef juices. Cover with a double thickness of baking paper, pressing it onto the surface of the liquid, then cover with the lid. Cook in the oven for 2 hours or until tender but still holding its shape. Pierce the meat with a fine skewer. It should offer no resistance; if not, continue cooking.

4 Remove the lid and paper, then leave to cool for 1 hour. Put the carrots and meat on separate plates and degrease the cooking liquor thoroughly with paper towel. Return the meat to the cooking liquor and leave to cool. Cover and refrigerate.

5 Put the cooled oyster blade on a plate, then remove the twine, pork skin and herbs. Dice some pork skin to yield about 1 cup.

6 Remove any traces of fat from the cooking liquor. Transfer 250ml of the cooking liquor to a small saucepan, then reduce over high heat to 40ml, skimming as it boils. Leave to cool.

7 To make the vinaigrette, mix the oil, reduced cooking liquor and vinegar with salt and pepper; you are after a decided acid finish so adjust with vinegar if necessary.

8 Using a sharp knife, cut the oyster blade lengthwise into 4 pieces, then cut each piece into 4 or 5 sections along its length. Using your fingertips, tear each section into threads. Moisten the beef generously with the vinaigrette and gently toss with your hands. Cut the carrots into 1cm slices.

9 To make the salad, combine all the ingredients in a large mixing bowl and moisten with three-quarters of the vinaigrette, then toss gently. Arrange on a platter. Toss with the beef, then moisten with the remaining vinaigrette and serve.

3 × 300g packets herring fillets in oil, drained and rinsed [preferably Eskal-brand Matjes]

3 eggs, at fridge temperature, pricked with a pin

1½ crisp eating apples, washed, cored and halved

juice of ½ lemon

3–4 tablespoons light sour cream

1 red onion, thinly sliced into rings

Herring marinade

3 teaspoons whole cloves

3 teaspoons whole allspice

4 small bay leaves

1 tablespoon white peppercorns

40ml Worcestershire sauce

330g white sugar

650ml good-quality white-wine vinegar

3 tablespoons prepared horseradish* [not the cream style]

160ml very dry sherry [such as Fino]

A Danish Herring & Potato Salad

The Scandinavians have a wide repertoire of dishes using herrings, a staple of their cuisine. In the late 1970s I worked as executive chef of the Sydney restaurant Pavilion on the Park. The Danish owner and chef, Mogens Bay Esbensen, introduced me to a little part of this culinary culture.

The herrings should marinate for at least a month before using to develop their full flavour.

1 To make the herring marinade, place the cloves, allspice, bay leaves, peppercorns, Worcestershire sauce, sugar and vinegar in a stainless-steel saucepan, then bring to the boil. Reduce the heat to low and simmer for 10 minutes. Remove from the heat, then add the horseradish and sherry and leave to cool completely at room temperature.

2 Scald a glass preserving jar with a non-metallic lid or airtight plastic container with boiling water, then dry with a clean tea towel. Transfer the cooled sherry mixture to the jar. Pat the herrings dry with paper towel, then add to the cooled marinade and refrigerate. The herring must be submerged in the marinade.

3 To make the sauce suédoise, put the apple and wine in a small saucepan. Simmer over low heat for a few minutes or until the apple is softened but still holds its shape. Drain, reserving the cooking liquor. Reduce the cooking liquor over high heat until you have 20ml, then leave to cool. Dry the apple with paper towel.

Sauce suédoise

1½ crisp eating apples, peeled, cored and cut into 3mm dice

100ml dry white wine

250ml very thick Mayonnaise* [made without mustard, using 3 egg yolks and 200ml vegetable oil]

1 tablespoon prepared horseradish* [this may be the cream style], or to taste

sea salt and freshly ground white pepper

a touch lemon juice [optional]

Potato salad

24 chat potatoes

60ml light olive oil

10–20 ml cider vinegar*

sea salt and freshly ground white pepper

½ head radicchio, washed and spin-dried, finely shaved

½ bunch chives, finely chopped

2 tablespoons small salted capers, soaked in warm water, rinsed and dried

Serves 6–8

4 Combine the reduced wine, apple, mayonnaise and horseradish to a coating consistency, then season with salt and pepper and finish with lemon juice if needed. Cover and refrigerate.

5 Meanwhile, hard-boil the eggs in a saucepan of simmering water for 9 minutes, refresh under cold running water then remove the shell.

6 To make the potato salad, plunge the potatoes into a saucepan of boiling salted water and simmer over medium heat for 20 minutes or until tender. Drain and leave to cool. Whisk the oil and vinegar with salt and pepper to make the vinaigrette.

7 Cut the potatoes in half, season lightly and moisten with vinaigrette, then toss gently. When they are cold, fold in the radicchio, chives and capers.

8 Drain as many herring fillets as required, discarding any spices. Shell the eggs and cut them in half lengthwise. Cut the halved apples into 3mm-thick slices and toss in the lemon juice, then drain and dry.

9 Distribute the potato salad between 6 flat plates, then place half an egg on top of each one. Curl the herring fillets close to the potato salad, placing 2 teaspoons sour cream in the centre. Tuck a few apple slices here and there and top with onion rings.

10 Drizzle the sauce suédoise over the herring and serve.

Sweet Salads

Salades sucrées

450g white sugar

900ml cold water

½ vanilla bean, split lengthwise, seeds scraped

3 strips scrubbed lime zest

ice cubes

8 slightly under-ripe yellow or white slipstone peaches

20–40ml kirsch

lime juice, to taste

300g raspberries

Serves 6

Salad of Peaches & Raspberries

The master chef of haute cuisine, August Escoffier, brought these flavours together when he created Peach Melba in 1893 to honour Dame Nellie Melba, the renowned opera singer. He used a peeled raw white peach clothed in a raspberry coulis sitting on a bed of vanilla ice cream. The simplicity of this dish is the essence of its perfection.

The trouble with using raw peaches is the discolouration that occurs almost immediately after they are cut, so now the peaches are generally poached in sugar syrup ahead of time. This salad uses sliced poached slipstone peaches and raspberries laced with some of the peach and lime syrup and a little kirsch.

1 Place the sugar, water, vanilla bean and scraped seeds and lime zest in a saucepan large enough to hold all the peaches in one layer. Stir over low heat to dissolve the sugar, taking care that the sugar is dissolved before the syrup boils.

2 Meanwhile, bring another pan of water to the boil and have a bowl of iced water at the ready. Make a tiny incision in the skin of each peach and lower it into the boiling water for 30 seconds or so until the skin begins to split. Transfer immediately to a bowl of iced water. The skins should slip off easily. Place each peeled peach directly in the hot sugar syrup, then cover the surface with a sheet of baking paper.

3 Poach gently for 10 minutes, then test for tenderness by piercing with a fine skewer; chances are they will require more time but this allows you to gauge the degree of cooking. Don't overcook the peaches; they should still be a touch firm. Remove the peaches from the heat, then carefully transfer them to a dish so that they don't touch each other [this is to preserve their shape]. Press plastic film over each peach to keep it from blemishing while it cools to room temperature, then refrigerate. Retain the poaching syrup.

4 Remove the vanilla bean and cut it into 6 fine matchsticks. Transfer 250ml of the poaching syrup into a bowl and leave to cool. Add the kirsch to the bowl, then finish with sufficient lime juice to freshen the flavour. Chill thoroughly. [Leftover syrup can be stored in the fridge for up to 1 week and used to poach other fruits.]

5 Holding a peach in one hand, slice it in half following the natural indent, then remove the stone. Retain 6 halves for presentation, then slice the remaining halves into 4 segments each. Distribute the peach slices between 6 chilled plates and place the halves in the centre of each plate, rounded-side up. Moisten with the syrup and scatter the raspberries over the peach. Place a few vanilla matchsticks on top of each peach half and chill in the fridge. Serve very cold.

8 small blood oranges
60g white sugar, or to taste
500g strawberries, hulled
20ml kirsch or a little less Cointreau
8 mint leaves
1 papaya
Serves 6

Papaya, Blood Orange &
Strawberry Salad

This is a salad for the winter months when blood oranges and good papaya are available. The sweetness of the papaya is cut by the acidity of the blood oranges and the strawberries are given a boost of flavour by being marinated in blood orange syrup [since they generally lack flavour at this time of the year]. A touch of mint adds a fresh finish to this attractive salad.

1   Remove the zest of 2 of the oranges with a vegetable peeler, avoiding the pith as much as possible, then cut into fine matchsticks. Place in a small saucepan of cold water and bring to the boil; drain and repeat this step. Drain and refresh under cold running water, then drain again. Pat dry with paper towel.

2   Reserve 2 oranges for their juice and proceed as follows with the remainder. Using a very sharp paring knife, cut a thin slice crosswise from the tops and bottoms of the oranges. Place a cut surface on a chopping board and allow the knife to follow the contour of the fruit between the flesh and pith; just take your time and aim for a smoothly rounded finish with no pith. Turn an orange onto its side and cut into 1cm-thick slices. Collect any juice that results from this process. Transfer the orange slices to a covered bowl for the moment.

3   Squeeze the juice from the 2 reserved oranges, adding any collected juice, then strain into a small saucepan; you need 200ml. Add the sugar and stir over low heat until dissolved before the syrup comes to the boil. Simmer for a few minutes then taste, whisking in enough additional sugar to sweeten the syrup while retaining the acidic character of the blood oranges, then add the zest. Cool to room temperature.

4   Cut the strawberries in half if they are large. Transfer to a bowl and soak in the blood orange syrup and kirsch. Cover and refrigerate for 1 hour.

5   Meanwhile, roll the mint leaves into a tight cigar shape and shred them finely using a very sharp knife. Cover and refrigerate.

6   When the strawberries are ready, cut the papaya in half crosswise, then remove the seeds. Cut each half into 2cm slices and remove the skin. Cut the slices into 2cm × 2cm × 4cm batons or small triangles. Transfer to a large mixing bowl, then add the sliced oranges, strawberries and marinade. Fold them gently, preferably with your hands, then leave for 10 minutes before presenting the salad in a glass bowl if one is on hand. If time permits, refrigerate until very cold. Scatter with the shaved mint just before serving.

2 limes	
60g white sugar	
120ml water	
½ vanilla bean, split lengthwise, seeds scraped	
10–20ml Cointreau	
6–8 mandarins	
6–8 kiwifruit	
6 portions	

Mandarin & Kiwifruit Salad

The combination of citrus fruit and kiwifruit is a happy marriage of flavours, especially when enhanced with a lime sugar syrup and a touch of Cointreau. Serve this salad after a rich main course. Some good-quality purchased biscotti will make a lovely crisp contrast to the texture of the fruit.

1   Use a zester to remove the zest of 1 of the limes, then squeeze it for its juice.

2   Place the lime juice, sugar, water and vanilla bean and scraped seeds in a saucepan, then heat over low heat, stirring continuously to dissolve the sugar. Simmer for 2–3 minutes, then add the zest. Pour into a bowl to cool.

3   Add 10ml of the Cointreau to the cool syrup then juice the remaining lime and add a little to the syrup to taste. Adjust with more Cointreau if needed.

4   Peel the mandarins, then carefully peel off the pith with your fingertips and a paring knife. Remove the pips, then place the fruit in a bowl and moisten with some of the syrup.

5   Peel the kiwifruit with a vegetable peeler, applying gentle pressure so that the shape remains as close to the original as possible. Cut thinly and place in a circle in the centre of 6 deep plates [or arrange on a platter], finishing with the mandarin segments and the syrup. Chill well before serving.

250ml wild honey	1kg lychees, peeled, seeds removed
boiling water	500g cherries, stalks removed
600ml dry white wine	ice cubes
1 vanilla bean, split lengthwise, seeds scraped	5 white slipstone peaches
1 watermelon	4 large mangoes
1 honeydew melon	¼ cup mint leaves, torn into small pieces
1 large rockmelon [cantaloupe]	**Serves 10–12**

Mogens's Salad of Seven Fruits

Mogens Bay Esbensen was my business partner at Pavilion on the Park in the late 1970s, and later at Butlers restaurant. Mogens had a restaurant in Bangkok for seventeen years that was the first European restaurant in Thailand. Naturally, he gained enormous experience handling tropical fruit and subsequently published a wonderful book on the subject called *A Taste of the Tropics*, where his recipe for this dish first appeared in print. This is my version of the original recipe. Mogens suggests serving the salad in the watermelon shell but the salad also looks superb in a big glass bowl or wide glass vase. It is best suited to a buffet, although the quantities could easily be halved and served in individual portions.

1 Put the honey in a large mixing bowl, add a little boiling water, then whisk to dissolve the honey before adding the wine. Add the vanilla bean and scraped seeds to the syrup.

2 Cut across the watermelon, removing about the top one-third. Scoop out the flesh from both pieces of watermelon and use a parisienne cutter* to form balls, discarding the seeds, then transfer to a very large bowl. Set the bottom two-thirds of the watermelon shell aside for serving the salad.

3 Slice the honeydew and rockmelon in half, remove the seeds and use the parisienne cutter to form balls, then add to the watermelon with the lychees.

4 Remove the cherry stones with a cherry stoner, then add to the bowl of fruit.

5 Have a saucepan of water boiling as well as a bowl of cold water containing plenty of ice cubes ready for peeling the peaches. Make a tiny incision in the skin of each peach then lower, 2 at a time, into the boiling water for 30 seconds or so until the skin begins to split. Transfer immediately to the bowl of iced water. The skins should slip off easily.

6 Holding a peeled peach in one hand, slice it in half following the natural indent, then remove the stone. Slice each half into 4 wedges and place directly into the honey and wine syrup.

7 Slice the cheeks off the mangoes, then use a large metal spoon to detach the flesh by holding a mango cheek in one hand and using a scooping action, with pressure against the skin. Slice the flesh into thick ribbons and add to the peaches.

8 Combine all the fruit and syrup, preferably using your hands with a gentle folding action. Transfer to the watermelon shell, then cover and refrigerate for a few hours to allow the flavours to mingle. Garnish with the mint and serve.

6 oranges	
200g caster sugar	
¼ teaspoon freshly ground cardamom seeds, or to taste	
375ml pinot noir [one that is not too acidic]	
pure icing sugar [optional]	
750g small sweet strawberries, hulled	

Serves 6

Strawberry & Orange Salad in Red Wine Syrup

This simple salad looks exciting sitting in its rich red dressing. Try to source sweet strawberries for the best flavour. Serve in deep white entrée bowls for the best effect.

1 Peel 2 of the oranges with a vegetable peeler, avoiding the white pith, cut the peel into fine matchsticks, then place in small saucepan. Cover with cold water and slowly bring to the boil over low heat. Drain and repeat this step, then drain again and set aside.

2 Juice 1 of the peeled oranges into a small saucepan, then add 2 tablespoons of the caster sugar and the cardamom. Dissolve the sugar, stirring over low heat, then simmer for 2 minutes. Leave to cool to room temperature.

3 Cut a thin crosswise slice from the top and bottom of the remaining oranges. Sit an orange on a chopping board and using a sharp paring knife, run it as close as possible to the contour of the orange between the flesh and pith to keep the natural shape. Holding the orange in one hand over a bowl, run the knife between each fillet and let it drop into the bowl. Do the same with the peeled but unjuiced orange. Drain the fillets and combine with the orange and cardamom syrup.

4 Combine the wine and remaining caster sugar in a saucepan and stir over low heat to dissolve the sugar. Simmer for 15 minutes to make a rich sauce. Taste, adding some sifted icing sugar if the syrup is too acidic. Cool to room temperature before pouring over the strawberries, then refrigerate until cold.

5 To serve, distribute the strawberries between 6 deep plates or bowls and moisten them with the red wine syrup. Scatter equally with the orange fillets, the syrup and reserved zest, then serve very cold.

60g white sugar

150ml water

40ml orange juice

juice of 1 lime, or to taste

60ml Campari

9 ripe nectarines, carefully washed and dried

36 large red seedless grapes, washed and
halved lengthwise

Serves 6

Nectarine & Grape Salad with Campari

I love the incredible sweet juiciness and perfume of nectarines. The acidity of the grapes and the aromatic flavour of Campari make this a delicious salad. Serve it in large wine glasses.

1   Place the sugar, water and citrus juice in a saucepan and stir over low heat to dissolve the sugar, taking care that the sugar is dissolved before the syrup boils, then simmer for 2 minutes. Pour into a bowl to cool. When cold, add the Campari, then taste, adding more lime juice if it is too sweet. Refrigerate until really cold.

2   Slice each nectarine into 6 wedges, depending on their size, directly into the cold syrup, then add the grapes. Cover and chill for 1 hour before serving in wine glasses or a glass bowl.

12 ripe but not too soft figs, chilled

juice and finely grated zest of 1 blood orange or navel orange

40ml Amaro Averna

icing sugar, to taste

1 small honeydew melon or champagne melon, chilled

24 Amaretti di Saronno

Serves 6

Fig & Honeydew Melon Salad with Crushed Amaretti

This simple combination of flavours and textures is best made at the last minute to preserve the texture of the amaretti biscuits. These very dry, crunchy Italian biscuits are flavoured with almonds and ground apricot kernels. If you have trouble finding the amaretti, then replace them with 120g toasted flaked almonds. Amaro is an aromatic spirit with a bitter finish and is generally served after the meal to aid the digestion. I have used blood orange juice for some acidity. While honeydew melon is excellent, try to find a champagne melon as it has a crisper texture and fresher flavour that offers a better contrast in this salad; rockmelon [cantaloupe] may also be used.

1 Wipe the figs with damp paper towel, then cut in half lengthwise, keeping the stalks intact if possible. Lay them cut-side up on a platter.

2 Combine the blood orange juice and zest with the Amaro and taste; it will need a little sweetening with the icing sugar [don't overdo it since the bitter quality of the Amaro is essential to this salad].

3 Moisten the figs lightly with the syrup.

4 Cut the melon in half, then remove the seeds and slice off the skin. Slice each half into 2cm-thick slices, then into batons or small diamonds. Arrange on serving plates with the figs, then drizzle with the remaining syrup.

5 Using a rolling pin, gently crack each biscuit into 2–3 pieces and scatter over the salad. Serve immediately.

1½ small rockmelons [cantaloupes]

60ml verjuice*

40–60ml mild honey, or to taste

6 large passionfruit, halved, the seeds and pulp scooped into a small bowl

450g raspberries

Serves 6

Rockmelon & Raspberry Salad with Honey & Passionfruit

This salad looks splendid in a wide glass bowl. It's an easy and quick salad, and while the ingredients can be prepared in advance, it should be assembled pretty much at the last minute to retain the freshness of the fruit. Excellent to serve as part of a summer menu, perhaps following a large baked whole fish served with a saffron pilaf and a green leaf salad such as the Green Goddess Salad [see page 71].

1   Cut a thin slice from the base of the rockmelon so that it will sit on a chopping board. Slice off all the skin, then cut in half and remove the seeds with a spoon.

2   Cut the melon into 2cm dice. Transfer it to a mixing bowl and moisten with the verjuice. Toss gently using your hands to minimise damaging the fruit. Cover with plastic film and refrigerate for 2 hours at most.

3   Melt the honey in a small heatproof bowl over another bowl of boiling water.

4   If the passionfruit pulp is of the type that sticks together, use 2 forks to break it up, then combine it with sufficient warm honey to sweeten without overwhelming its flavour.

5   To serve, transfer half the rockmelon with its liquid to a glass serving bowl or glass coupes, then moisten evenly with half the honey and passionfruit dressing. Scatter half the raspberries over the fruit then repeat with the remaining fruit and dressing. Chill well before serving very cold.

12 small Turkish dried figs	1 vanilla bean, split lengthwise, seeds scraped
18 large prunes, pitted	3 cloves
boiling water, for soaking	4 white peppercorns, lightly cracked
6 blood oranges or 4 of another variety of orange [blood oranges are usually small]	300g white sugar
	350ml cold water
1 lemon	**Serves 6**

A Dried & Citrus Fruit Salad

We used to serve this salad at Claude's to accompany a hazelnut parfait. The principal ingredients of dried figs and prunes are cooked in an aromatic sugar syrup that is given a touch of freshness by the addition of orange and lemon zests and orange fillets. One could serve this with a dollop of very lightly whipped sweetened mascarpone flavoured with a little vanilla extract, with toasted chopped hazelnuts folded through. Remember to oven-toast the nuts initially to loosen their skins, then to rub the nuts in a sieve with a cloth to detach the skins. This is a lovely dessert to follow a rich dish such as braised oxtail.

1   Cover the figs and prunes with boiling water and leave them to swell for 15 minutes or so.

2   Remove the zest from 2 of the oranges and the lemon using a vegetable peeler, avoiding the white pith, and cut into fine matchsticks. Place the zest in a small saucepan of cold water and bring to the boil slowly over low heat. Drain and repeat this step, then drain again. Juice these oranges and the lemon into a medium saucepan, adding the vanilla bean and scraped seeds. Wrap the cloves and peppercorns in a little muslin bag, then tie with kitchen twine.

3   Add the sugar and cold water to the saucepan and bring to the boil over low heat, stirring to dissolve the sugar, then simmer for 5 minutes. Add the drained figs and prunes and simmer over low heat for 15 minutes. The prunes may be cooked now and should be transferred to a plate while the figs continue cooking until tender [if the dried figs are not fresh they will need extra time].

4   Meanwhile, remove and discard the zest from the remaining oranges. Cut a thin crosswise slice from the top and bottom of the oranges. Sit an orange on a chopping board and, using a sharp paring knife, run it as close as possible to the contour of the orange to keep the natural shape. Holding the orange in one hand over a bowl, run the knife between each fillet and let it drop into the bowl with any juice. Repeat with the remaining oranges.

5   Transfer the cooked fruit to a salad bowl with the syrup, discarding the muslin bag. Add the orange and lemon zest, then cool to room temperature before adding the orange fillets. Serve well chilled.

Glossary of Ingredients, Equipment & Techniques

This section explains some of the equipment and raw materials called for throughout this book. I have made suggestions as to suitable alternatives in both areas to simplify the difficulties often experienced in finding the right utensil or ingredient. To those cooks who buy every utensil they can to do the job perfectly, it should be noted that few commercial kitchens have every gadget and purpose-designed utensil in their *batterie de cuisine*. Professionals are often forced to compromise by using whatever is on hand principally because of the high cost and lack of storage space. I have also included some culinary terms of interest beyond those referred to in the text.

See also the list of Suppliers on page 217 for specific ingredients referred to in some recipes.

Acidulating

This refers to the addition of an acid, such as vinegar, citrus juice or verjuice to accentuate and balance richer flavours. Acidulated water is also used to prevent cut vegetables and fruit such as apples from discolouring.

Apple corer

A tubular device with a serrated cutting edge at its base that makes coring apples quick and easy. The apple corer is inserted into the top of apple and pushed down to the bottom to remove the core.

Armagnac

A brandy made in Gascony where it is produced both commercially and by specialist artisans. Armagnac is single-distilled while cognac is double-distilled.

Avocados

Store unripe avocados at room temperature in a brown paper bag to speed up maturation. To remove the seeds from avocado halves, cut down the length of the avocado in a continuous line from the stalk end to produce two halves. Hold the half containing the seed in the palm of one hand, then tap a sharp knife into the seed and twist slowly to remove it. To remove the skin, use a small knife to pull the skin away from the stalk end: it should come off easily if the avocado is ripe, although with some varieties the skin breaks at random, making this a fiddly process. If only one half is required, store the other with the stone still attached [sealed in plastic film] as this technique inhibits discolouration.

Banyuls

Refers to a red-wine vinegar made in the Roussillon commune which is part of the Languedoc region of France, located to the east of the Pyrenees. This vinegar has a lovely balance between sweet and acidic flavours. [See also Suppliers.]

Blanching

The name given to a technique of briefly plunging an ingredient into boiling salted water, such as when cooking green vegetables, but it can also refer to the process whereby an ingredient is placed in cold water and then brought to the boil. Garlic, for example, is sometimes blanched from a cold-water start to soften its flavour, and this may be repeated several times until the desired result is achieved. A similar technique is used for purifying – for example, to release congealed blood from chicken carcasses when making stock, or to extract some of the saltiness from corned beef or other pickled meats.

Bouquet Garni

A bundle of aromatics composed of fresh thyme, parsley stalks, bay leaves, lemon zest as well as other flavourings that may complement a particular dish; traditionally, a bouquet garni often included celery stalk. The contents are wrapped in muslin cloth and tied with kitchen twine or simply tied together.

Brains

Lambs' and calves' brains are peeled using the same method. Soak them in cold water for 1 hour then using fingertips, carefully pull away the membrane and blood vessels and soak again for another hour before poaching.

Butter

Unsalted butter is generally used for cooking in France since it does not burn as readily as the salted product. I think is lends a more authentic French taste to dishes we cook in Australia. [See also 'Clarified Butter'.]

Candy Thermometer

See 'Thermometers'.

Chargrill

Cast-iron chargrills are a good alternative to a wood-fired barbecue for cooking meat, poultry and game as well as fish, scallops and prawns. These grills are well suited for cooking thin slices of eggplant and zucchini, radicchio leaves and lightly blanched asparagus since there is no direct contact with fire.

Cider, Seaweed, Eschalot & Fleur de Sel Vinegar

This is a unique product from Collonges-la-Rouge in Limousin, France. Seaweed, eschalots and marine herbs are steeped in a high-quality cider vinegar, then seasoned with fleur de sel salt [see page TBA]. Delicious with freshly shucked oysters, in a fish-based reduction or with cooked green beans.

Cider Vinegar

Vinegars are produced by allowing wine to come into contact with air, which permits airborne bacteria to oxidise the wine or, in this case, alcoholic cider. Cider vinegar has a lovely balance of flavour and fruity acidity.

Clarified Butter

This is the preferred cooking medium in the French kitchen because the absence of milk solids [resulting from the clarification process] inhibits the fat from burning as readily as fresh butter.

The technique for clarifying butter is very easy. Simply melt unsalted butter over low heat and allow it to simmer until the solids fall to the bottom of the pan. This may take a little time but don't be tempted to leave it unattended since the solids may burn. Strain

the butter through a fine sieve lined with muslin into small sealable containers, cool to room temperature, then refrigerate for up to a few months.

Cooling Food

It is important that food be cooled as quickly as possible to avoid contamination from harmful bacteria and other microbes. The 'danger zone', as it is known, is between 10°C and 65°C.

While the obvious solution is to pop the hot food into the fridge, this is really asking for trouble! This causes the food [especially liquids] to cool quickly on the outside while the centre remains locked in the 'danger zone' and additionally, other food in the fridge such as eggs may absorb the unwanted flavours from the hot food. The negative results may not always be obvious or disastrous, especially in strongly flavoured dishes such as curries.

The practical solution is to cool the food in a wide bowl set over another bowl containing ice and highly salted water [or spread cooked minced meat products in a roasting tin suspended over a cake-cooling rack]. The food has a large surface area exposed to hasten its cooling. Stir the food regularly to speed up the process, then press a piece of plastic film onto the surface and refrigerate.

Always thoroughly chill food intended to be frozen before storing it in the freezer. Pressing plastic film onto the surface before sealing the container with a lid inhibits the formation of crystallised vapor in the space between the food and the lid. Always thaw frozen food slowly in the fridge, if practicable, since this produces the best tasting result when reheated. Never refreeze thawed food, particularly chicken, as the water retained around the joints can harbour harmful bacteria, such as salmonella, which then multiply during the freezing process. Prawns in particular must not be refrozen since virtually all prawns are snap-frozen when harvested.

Confit

A term principally used to describe pork, goose and duck, first salted then cooked very slowly, traditionally in goose fat or lard, to preserve it. For a lighter result, substitute olive or vegetable oil for animal fat; this is particularly suitable for fish, shellfish and vegetables.

Cornichons

Small pickled cucumbers often served with charcuterie. Their high level of acidity makes them suitable for sharpening the flavour of mayonnaise-based sauces such as tartare sauce. Cornichons are particularly useful in balancing flavours in salads containing richly flavoured ingredients and may even play the role of vinegar to refresh the palate structure of a dish.

Crème Fraîche

A French dairy product that has had a lactic bacterium introduced to make it thicker and give it a nutty, slightly acidic character. Crème fraîche adds an authentic quality to French cooking, particularly sauces.

Deep-frying

Successful deep-frying calls for a purpose-designed deep-fryer or a deep, wide-based pan and a candy thermometer [see 'Thermometers'] to monitor the temperature of the oil. Specially designed utensils, such as those made from coiled tinned wire or stainless steel are best for lifting the finished product from the fryer. Drain the food on folded paper towel and dust with salt before serving.

Déglaçage

The term given to the sediment released from the base of a pan by the process of deglazing [see below].

Deglazing

The practice of adding verjuice,※ wine, vinegar, stock or water to pan sediments in order to capture their flavour as the foundation for a sauce or vinaigrette. The sediments are dislodged using a flat wooden spoon to scrape the base of the pan. The resultant liquid is called 'déglaçage'.

Eggs – Poaching

It is best to use very fresh eggs for poaching since the whites congeal more readily around the yolk. The addition of 1 teaspoon white-wine vinegar to 1.5 litres water helps to form a neatly shaped poached egg. I like to break the egg into a small cup or ramekin which assists in achieving a good rounded shape. Specially designed poaching boats made by Claystone Pottery

[see Suppliers] are particularly good for slipping an egg into the poaching water.

Bring the water and vinegar to a rolling boil then slip the egg into the saucepan close to the edge. The rolling action of the boiling water at the side of the pan helps to form the right shape immediately. Reduce the heat a little and poach for 2½ minutes for a soft yolk if using 60g eggs. Retrieve the egg using a slotted spoon and lay on a folded clean tea towel to drain, then pat the surface dry. If you wish to cook the eggs ahead of time, simply transfer them from the pan to a bowl of iced water to arrest further cooking. To reheat, slip the egg back into near boiling water for 30 seconds, remove and then dry as above. Poach 2 eggs at a time for the best results.

Filleting Citrus

This technique also pertains to most varieties of citrus fruit. Cut a thin slice form the top and bottom of the fruit and place a cut-side down on a chopping board. Use a small very sharp knife to remove the skin and pith by running it from top to bottom in a smooth action following the natural contour of the fruit. The fruit should have a smooth rounded surface similar to its original shape and be free of pith. To cut slices, turn the fruit on its side and slice to the desired thickness.

To achieve fillets, cradle the fruit in one hand with the side facing upwards. Using a paring knife, slice between the pith and flesh to produce pith-less segments. This operation is best done over a bowl to collect the juice. Remove any pips with a flick of the knife or with your fingers.

Fines Herbes

A mixture of fresh herbs consisting of tarragon, chervil, parsley and chives used to flavour mayonnaise, vinaigrettes and hot sauces. Fines herbes are very useful in salads.

Florets

Also called fleurettes, meaning 'little flowers' in French. Pertains to the tiny individual heads cut from cauliflower and broccoli heads. They are delicious to eat raw in a salad, particularly as an ingredient in a vegetable salad dressed with a Thai dressing consisting of garlic, chilli, sugar, fish sauce and lime juice. The dressing should taste spicy, hot, sweet and sour. Plunge into boiling salted water for a minute or two, then refresh under cold running water if called for in a European recipe.

Foie Gras

This is the French word used to describe the fattened livers of ducks and geese. A typical whole foie gras may weigh up to one kilogram. Foie gras is not produced in Australia and imports are restricted to preserved livers. Quarantine regulations require a specific degree of cooking to kill certain bacteria that may introduce diseases. [See also Suppliers.]

Food Processor

This machine revolutionised commercial and domestic cooking when it was launched on the French food service market in the 1960s. These days most manufacturers of electric appliances offer a food processor in their range but I believe Cuisinart to be the best available domestic machine.

The belief that all manner of food may be processed successfully in one of these machines is dubious. For example, onions chopped in a food processor become bitter almost immediately. These machines are unsuitable for chopping or mincing meat destined for a terrine or sauce. Conversely, they make excellent purées of liver for a pâté and vegetables purées [with the exception of potatoes, since the starch becomes glue-like and destroys the texture]. I rarely use a food processor for making mayonnaise unless it is based on a purée of leaf vegetables or herbs. The best mayonnaise is hand-made using a whisk or wooden spoon, since the rapid action of the machine tends to destroy the individual flavours of the ingredients. The texture of machine-made mayonnaise tends to be very tight and lacks the naturally unctuous quality associated with this emulsion sauce.

Forum Cabernet & Forum Chardonnay Vinegars

These complex vinegars come from the Bai Penedes region near Barcelona in Spain. They are made from a high-quality wine base and slowly acidified using an artisanal method similar to the one used in the Spanish solera system for making sherry.

The cabernet variety has a bittersweet quality and marries well with freshly shucked oysters, vinaigrettes and in reductions for sauces.

The chardonnay style has a smooth, sweet-sour flavour that is particularly good as a flavouring for fish and shellfish and in vinaigrettes.

Ground Rice

Long-grain rice such as jasmine that has been toasted until very slightly coloured, then cooled and ground to a powder. A common ingredient in many Asian cuisines. Its role is to add texture and a nutty taste to a dish.

Halen Môn Pure Sea Salt

This flaked salt comes from Wales in the United Kingdom and has a very distinct flavour; the smoked variety is especially interesting. Ideal to finish a salad or food that calls for a dusting of salt to bring out its full flavour.

Herbes de Provence

Available ready-prepared, herbes de Provence is a blend of dried mountain herbs generally consisting of wild thyme, savory, parsley, marjoram or oregano, lavender and bay leaves.

Horseradish

Very few prepared horseradish products can compare with the freshly grated root. Grating by hand will result in tears but for those who have a fruit juice extractor, the process is quick and avoids the tears. Simply peel away the skin and pass the roots through the machine, collecting the juice in a small jug. Combine the grated flesh and juice, then season with salt and a touch of lemon juice to arrest discoloration. Press the contents into a small jar, cover the top with a thin layer of vegetable oil, then refrigerate.

Prepared horseradish is readily available in supermarkets and specialty food stores. The most common version is grated and seasoned and usually contains an antioxidant. The creamed variety is generally milder.

Knives – Sharpening

Sharp knives can make a real difference to the quality of food presentation and the time spent in the kitchen. Knives are only useful tools if they are kept sharp, so invest in a professional sharpening stone. It is easy to master the sharpening technique: the blade is passed back and forth with mild pressure across the stone at a slight angle until sharp [just follow the manufacturer's instructions]. Maintaining a sharp cutting edge requires regular honing with a steel. I find diamond steels to be the best: they are not outrageously expensive and are likely to last a lifetime in a domestic kitchen. Always moisten a diamond steel under running water before use.

Mandoline

This is among the most useful and time-saving pieces of cooking equipment. A mandoline is invaluable for making onion rings and slicing most hard root vegetables, including fennel bulbs. Always use the hand-held guard and position the bottom of the device on a folded damp cloth for stability. Be especially vigilant when slicing hard vegetables like celeriac – excessive pressure should not be necessary and may cause the mandoline to move, possibly resulting in a nasty cut to your hand.

Mayonnaise

This is an emulsion sauce that is best made by hand in a bowl, preferably a narrow, tallish one, using a wire whisk or wooden spoon. It should take about 5 minutes to make 500ml if the ingredients are at room temperature. The key to success is to add the oil slowly, adding more oil once the previous amount has been absorbed.

Put 2 egg yolks into a bowl with a ¼ teaspoon salt, some pepper and 1 teaspoon Dijon-style mustard, if desired. Combine with a whisk, then gradually add the first addition of oil, initially drop by drop and then in a thin, steady stream. When the ingredients look emulsified, that is, the mixture looks smooth, add some more oil. Continue with 300–400 ml oil, using about one-third extra virgin olive oil to two-thirds grapeseed or other vegetable oil. The mayonnaise should be quite thick and have a dull sheen by now. Acidulate to taste with lemon juice or white-wine vinegar, then correct the seasoning to taste. Refrigerate the mayonnaise in a sealed container with a piece of plastic film or greaseproof paper placed directly on the surface of the sauce. It should keep for at least 1 week.

Microplane

This is the best grating device I have ever used. A wide range is available offering varying apertures for grating all manner of food from hard parmesan cheese to chocolate. I find a Microplane grater especially good for citrus zest, as the essential oils are retained.

Mortar & Pestle

Purists would insist that this is the only way to grind spices and I would have to agree. The pestle, a round-headed hammer that fits the shape of the mortar, does the job of grinding; the action is not one of pounding, but rather a rotary movement within the mortar that gradually reduces the spices to a powder. When buying a mortar and pestle, look for a large one, preferably made of stone. It's a good idea to place a damp cloth underneath for stability.

Mouli-légumes & Mouli-julienne

Mouli is a French manufacturer of small kitchen gadgets, originally manually operated but increasingly power-driven these days. A Mouli-légumes is a mill for making vegetable purées and is indispensable in any kitchen.

A Mouli-julienne is designed to shred, slice and grate vegetables, nuts and hard cheese. I have one at home that I bought 20 years ago, and I still use it to produce perfect grated carrots for that very French salad of grated carrots seasoned with olive oil and lemon juice [see page 63]. Regrettably, I have not seen this model in stores for some years so it may not be available any more – keep an eye out for one at garage sales.

Mudcrabs

To boil a mudcrab, place the live creature in the freezer for 30–45 minutes then bring it out. Add 250 g white sugar and 250 g pure salt to 5–6 litres cold water and bring to the boil, stirring to dissolve the sugar as the water heats. When condensation appears on the crab's shell, lower it into the boiling solution and simmer for 18 minutes per kilogram.

Remove to a sink and cool under cold running water for a few minutes. Crack the cap of the body and each joint of the claws using the blunt edge of a cleaver, a meat mallet or, best of all, a rolling pin, then turn upside-down to drain in a colander. If shelling is to be postponed, be sure the crab has cooled thoroughly before refrigerating.

Mustard fruits – Mostarda di Frutta [di Cremona]

Several varieties of fruit are used for this preserve such as figs, pears and melon. The fruit is candied in a sugar and honey syrup flavoured with mustard oil. The original comes from Cremona but other regions of Italy have their own specific types of mostarda.

Omelette

A splendid omelette is very easy to make and is ready in a minute or so. A heavy-based non-stick frying pan removes the possibility of the omelette sticking to the surface. Break two or three eggs into a small bowl, then add 1 tablespoon heavy cream or crème fraîche and season with salt and pepper. Use a fork to break up the yolks but don't beat the mixture. Heat the pan until really hot over high heat, then add a nut of butter [ideally, clarified]. When the butter is very hot, pour in the egg mixture and allow a few seconds for the omelette to begin to set. Using both a shaking technique and a rubber or wooden spatula, pull away the cooked mixture, tilting the pan so that the raw egg comes into contact with the heat of the pan. Now add a chosen filling such as crabmeat or skinned, seeded and diced tomato, then use the spatula to round off an inner edge of the omelette. Do the same on the other side, forming rounded 'pinched' ends. Hold the pan underneath the handle on a 45-degree angle to a plate, at a similar angle, then gently slide the omelette onto the plate.

Paprika – Hot Smoked

This is a Spanish specialty product that has a complex, slightly sweet character and gentle spiciness. It marries well with squid in particular and adds complexity to a vinaigrette. It should be ever so lightly toasted in a dry pan over low heat for 30 seconds or so until aromatic if used in a dressing or for dusting over a salad. [See also Suppliers.]

Parisienne Cutter

This handy tool is also known as a 'melon baller' and is used for cutting tiny balls from fruit and vegetables. It is a very useful tool for removing the cores from apples and pears. A larger tool based on the same design is called a 'noisette' cutter since it refers to the size of the ball being close to that of a hazelnut.

Sauce Vierge

The word *vierge* means 'virgin' or 'pure' in French. This very useful sauce is based on extra virgin olive oil with the addition of peeled, seeded and diced tomato and fresh herbs such as tarragon, chervil and chives, seasoned with salt and freshly ground pepper.

Spatchcock

This is a young chicken weighing 400-500g.

The term 'spatchcock' relates to the technique of splitting the bird from the back so that it may be flattened ready for grilling. The easiest way to do this is with the aid of poultry shears. Turn the bird onto its breast and cut on either side of the back bone and put aside, perhaps to be used for a stock. Use both hands to gently pull on both sides to partially open the chicken. Place on a chopping board and press the breast firmly with both hands until you hear a creaking sound; turn over and make a very shallow incision on ether side of the bone dividing the breasts. The spatchcock may now be marinated briefly in oil seasoned with rosemary, garlic, salt and pepper and then grilled under a fairly brisk overhead griller or on a cast-iron chargrill or barbecue.

Stainless-steel Skewers

I find a fine skewer the most useful instrument to test when vegetables are cooked. Because it is thin I can feel the texture within a potato more accurately than with a paring knife. Before the invention of the meat 'probe' thermometer [see 'Thermometers' below], a skewer was used to test the doneness of cooked meat by inserting it into the thickest part of the piece. After 30 seconds the internal temperature was transmitted to the skewer, which the cook placed on his or her lower lip to register.

Thermometers

I find thermometers invaluable in certain recipes for maintaining consistency and food safety. A simple candy thermometer is useful to gauge the temperature of oil used for deep-frying and for controlling the temperature of a poaching liquid. 'Probe' thermometers help the cook to achieve the perfect result when roasting meat. Food thermometers are available from specialist cookware shops.

Tomatoes

I have referred to specific varieties of tomato that I feel are best suited to particular recipes throughout this book. We are fortunate to have several varieties to choose from these days thanks to both hydroponic and glasshouse cultivation methods now widely used by farmers. While these methods produce wonderful results, they sometimes lack the full flavour associated with naturally grown tomatoes. The Roma variety is generally reliable and available throughout the year. Ox or Bullock Heart, Black Russian or Kumatoes, cherry and truss, as well as vine-ripened are all excellent for salads. A particularly great cultivar is marketed as 'Love Bite' and, at the time of writing, is available only from Fratelli Fresh stores in Sydney [see Suppliers].

To peel a tomato, cut a little shallow cross in the top then blanch by lowering into boiling water for ten seconds. Transfer it to iced water with a slotted spoon, then gently squeeze off the skin. Pat dry with paper towel.

Tuna – Tinned [e.g. Crespi and Ortiz]

Bottled and tinned tuna fillets are often overlooked as being inferior to the fresh product. However, brands such Spanish Ortiz [available from Simon Johnson stores, see Suppliers] or Italian Crespi [available from Fratelli Fresh stores, see Suppliers] are really superior to supermarket versions. A true salade niçoise is made with bottled or tinned tuna [see page 65].

Verjuice

Made from the stabilised juice extracted from unripe grapes, verjuice has a soft acidic quality that enhances sauces and makes it perfect for deglazing pans after roasting or pan-frying. It has been used for centuries in French and other European cuisines; in Australia, Maggie and Colin Beer were the first to produce verjuice commercially and now export it to Japan, the United Kingdom and the United States.

Vino Cotto [or Vincotto]

In Italy this is primarily used as a seasoning. It is made in a similar way to balsamic vinegar. The must of Negromaro and Black Malvasia grapes is boiled very slowly, then matured in oak barrels with a vinegar 'mother'. Use it when you need a true sweet-and-sour flavour to highlight a salad such as one of beetroot, baby beetroot leaves and toasted walnuts, or in an extra virgin olive oil-based vinaigrette, with a little Forum Cabernet vinegar[*] added for complexity.

Fig vino cotto is obtained by adding a natural fig syrup to vino cotto after its third year of ageing. Sweet and complex, it has an affinity with roasted game and grilled duck breast.

Maggie Beer has Australian vino cotto and fig vino cotto in her range of products.

Suppliers

Here is a short list of shops I support for my domestic cooking needs.

Fruit & Vegetables

Fratelli Fresh
7 Danks Street, Waterloo NSW 2017
(02) 9699 3110

Shop 2/81 Macleay Street, Potts Point NSW 2011
(02) 9357 2940

Wholefoods House Organic Supermarket
9 Danks Street, Waterloo NSW 2017
(02) 9319 4459

109 Queen Street, Woollahra NSW 2025
(02) 9363 9879

Fourth Village Providore
5a Vista Street, Mosman NSW 2088
(02) 9960 7162

Grocery, Cheese & Imported Ingredients

Fratelli Fresh
See above [carries Crespi products]

Simon Johnson Purveyor of Quality Foods
24a Ralph Street, Alexandria NSW 2015
(02) 8244 8288

181 Harris Street, Pyrmont NSW 2007
(02) 9552 2522

55 Queen Street, Woollahra NSW 2025
(02) 9328 6888

Meat, Poultry & Game

Hudson Meats
Shop 1, 410 Crown Street, Surry Hills NSW 2010
(02) 9332 4454

Stockland Cammeray
450–476 Miller Street, Cammeray NSW 2062
(02) 9954 5900

Penny's Quality Butchery
880 Military Road, Mosman NSW 2088
(02) 9969 3372

Victor Churchill
132 Queen Street, Woollahra NSW 2025
(02) 9328 0402

Terry Wright's Gourmet Meats
32 Clovelly Road, Randwick NSW 2031
(02) 9398 1038

Fish & Shellfish

Sydney Fish Markets
There are several excellent suppliers within the market. I use Claudio's for my domestic needs.

Foie Gras

G J Foods
Unit 13, 5–13 Parsons Street, Rozelle NSW 2039
(02) 9555 7750

Simon Johnson Purveyor of Quality Foods
See above [also carries Ortiz products]

Spices

Herbie's Spices
745 Darling Street, Rozelle NSW 2039
(02) 9555 6035
herbie@herbies.com.au
They have an excellent mail-order service.

Cooking Equipment

Accoutrement
611 Military Road, Mosman NSW 2088
(02) 9969 1031
accoutrement.com.au

Chefs' Warehouse
111 Albion Street, Surry Hills NSW 2010
(02) 9211 4555

The Bay Tree
40 Queen Street, Woollahra NSW 2025
(02) 9328 1101

Claystone Pottery Poaching Boats
Richmond Hill Café and Larder
48–50 Bridge Road, Richmond Vic. 3121
(03) 9421 2808
Call to mail order

Props Suppliers

Camargue
545 Military Road, Mosman NSW 2088
(02) 9960 6234

Pavillon Christofle
11 Bay Street, Double Bay NSW 2028
(02) 9363 4110
christofle.com

Michael Green Antiques
108 Queen Street, Woollahra NSW 2025
(02) 9328 1712
michaelgreene.com.au

Hermès
135 Elizabeth Street, Sydney NSW 2000
(02) 9287 3200
hermes.com

Accoutrement
See page 217

JOHNANDPETER catering
127 Bondi Road
Bondi NSW 2026
(02) 9387 4544
johnandpeter.com

Anibou
726 Bourke Street
Redfern NSW 2016
(02) 9319 0655
anibou.com.au

Seneca Textiles
27 Boundary Street
Rushcutters Bay NSW 2011
(02) 9361 3099
senecatextiles.com

South Pacific Fabrics
195 Paddington St
Paddington NSW 2021
(02) 9327 7222
southpacificfabrics.com

Mokum Textiles
98 Barcom Ave
Rushcutters Bay NSW 2011
(02) 9357 0555
mokumtextiles.com

Bibliography

Alexander, Stephanie, *The Cook's Companion*, Viking, Melbourne, 1996.

——, *Cooking and Travelling in South-West France*, Viking, Melbourne, 2002.

Barker, Alex & Sallie Mansfield, *Potato: The Definitive Guide to Potatoes and Potato Cooking*, Lorenz Books, London, 1999.

Beer, Maggie, *Maggie's Farm*, Allen & Unwin, Sydney, 1993.

Beranbaum, Rose Levy, *The Cake Bible*, William Morrow, New York, 1988.

David, Elizabeth, *French Provincial Cooking*, Penguin, Harmondsworth, 1960.

Davidson, Alan, *The Penguin Companion to Food*, Penguin, London, 2002.

Ducasse, Alain, *Ducasse: Flavors of France*, Artisan, New York, 1998.

Escaudier, Jean Noël & Peta Fuller, *True Provençal and Niçoise Cooking*, Macmillan, London, 1971.

Escoffier, Georges Auguste, *A Guide to Modern Cookery*, Heinemann, London, 1965 (first published 1907).

Girardet, Fredy, *Cuisine Spontanée*, Macmillan, London, 1985.

Grigson, Jane, *Jane Grigson's English Food*, Macmillan, London, 1979.

——, *Jane Grigson's Vegetable Book*, Macmillan, London, 1980.

——, *Jane Grigson's Fruit Book*, Michael Joseph, London, 1982.

Guérard, Michel, *Michel Guérard's Cuisine Minceur*, Macmillan, London, 1977.

——, *Michel Guérard's Cuisine Gourmande*, Macmillan, London, 1978.

Hemphill, Ian, *Spice Notes: A Cook's Compendium of Herbs*, Pan Macmillan, Sydney, 2000.

Larousse Gastronomique, *The Concise Larousse Gastronomique: The World's Greatest Cookery Encyclopedia*, Hamlyn, London, 1998.

Leyel, Hilda & Olga Hartley, *The Gentle Art of Cookery*, Chatto & Windus, London, 1925.

McGee, Harold, *On Food and Cooking: The Science and Lore of the Kitchen*, Allen & Unwin, London, 1984.

Malouf, Greg & Lucy, *Arabesque: Modern Middle-Eastern Food*, Hardie Grant, Melbourne, 1999.

Olney, Richard, *Simple French Food*, Grub Street, London, 2003.

Pellaprat, Henri-Paul (edited by John Fuller), *L'Art Culinaire Moderne*, Collins, London, 1965.

Pépin, Jacques, *La Technique: The Fundamental Techniques of Cooking, an Illustrated Guide*, Macmillan, London, 1982.

——, *La Methode: An Illustrated Guide to the Fundamental Techniques of Cooking*, Macmillan, London, 1983.

Roux, Michel, *Sauces: Sweet and Savoury, Classic and New*, Viking, Melbourne, 1997.

Saulnier, L., *Le Répertoire de la Cuisine*, Leon Jaeggi & Sons, London, 1982 (first published 1914).

Schneider, Elizabeth, *Vegetables from Amaranth to Zucchini: The Essential Reference*, William Morrow, 2001.

Time-Life Books, *Salads & Cold Hors-d'Oeuvres*, Time-Life Books, Alexandria, Virginia, 1980.

Acknowledgements

With this book, Julie Gibbs, the highly respected publisher of my first book, *French*, commissioned a work that reflects my love of the broad and exciting genre within the French repertoire known as *salades*. Thank you, Julie, for the unique judgement you have brought to this, my second cookery book.

During my lifetime of cooking in Australia within the French culinary style, I have witnessed an amazing development in the availability of fine raw ingredients and, most importantly, a revolution in the palates of the dining public. As cooks, either domestic or professional, we embrace our preferred cuisines and attempt to replicate their flavours and style away from the homeland. As a matter of course, the results must be different – and this I believe is the strength we enjoy in Australia.

I have been so fortunate to know as well as work with several fine mentors, including Stephanie Alexander, Gay Bilson, Maggie Beer and Janni Kyritsis, to name a few. At the forefront are my mother's delicious food, which inspired me to cook, and the opportunities afforded by Mogens Bay Esbensen when he offered me the great challenge of taking on the role of executive chef of his highly acclaimed Pavilion on the Park in Sydney in 1978.

The masters of classic French cuisine, Auguste Escoffier and Henri Paul Pellaprat, provided my starting points, followed closely by the enlightened works of Elizabeth David, Jane Grigson and Richard Olney. But I am also indebted to the army of young chefs I have worked with, including Jason Roberts and Tom Walton, for the youthful freedom they have brought to my cooking and the many restaurants I have created.

Thanks to my friends and colleagues who generously gave me permission to use their recipes in this book: Sean Moran of Sean's Panaroma, Bondi Beach, NSW [page 29]; Stefano Manfredi of Bells at Killcare, Central Coast, NSW [page 66]; Kylie Kwong of Billy Kwong, Surry Hills, NSW [page 121]; Stephanie Puharich, NSW [page 123]; Alex Herbert, head chef and co-owner of Bird Cow Fish, Surry Hills, NSW [page 176]; and Neil Perry of Rockpool, Sydney and Melbourne [page 181].

I wish to thank my editor, Kathleen Gandy, for her great professionalism in making my words come to life in *Salades*. Thanks also to Nicola Young, and the Penguin/Lantern sales and marketing team, whose enthusiasm for the book will, I know, make it a success.

My friend Michael Fitzjames created the logo for Bistro Moncur that we used as the cover of *French*. Thank you, Michael, for creating another brilliant cover that reflects *Salades* so perfectly. Thanks to Vince Frost, who designed the original layout of *French*, for the reuse of his design in this elegant publication. Thanks go to the Penguin/Lantern designers Evi Oetomo, who perfected the layout, and Megan Pigott, who organised the photography shoot. Thanks, too, to Margot Braddon for the mountains of props she sourced for the *Salades* photographs.

To the photographer, Anson Smart, thank you for the brilliant times my loyal helper Jason Roberts and I spent working with your great talent to achieve such concise and beautiful images. Our hard work and great fun is so rewarded by your photographs for this book.

And thank you to my friends and business partners Ron and Robin White for their constant support and Karen Anderson for proof reading my recipes.

The following people and businesses most generously supplied props for the photographs: Sue Jenkins of Accoutrement, Mosman, NSW; Chris Hazell and Gill O'Brien of Chefs' Warehouse, Surry Hills, NSW; Michael Green Antiques, Woollahra, NSW; The Bay Tree, Woollahra, NSW; Pavillon Christofle, Double Bay, NSW; Hermès Paris, Sydney, NSW; Camargue, Mosman, NSW; JOHNANDPETER catering, Bondi, NSW; Anibou, Redfern, NSW; and Ron and Robin White.

Index

P

W

LANTERN

Published by the Penguin Group
Penguin Group [Australia]
250 Camberwell Road, Camberwell, Victoria 3124, Australia
[a division of Pearson Australia Group Pty Ltd]
Penguin Group [USA] Inc.
375 Hudson Street, New York, New York 10014, USA
Penguin Group [Canada]
90 Eglinton Avenue East, Suite 700, Toronto ON M4P 2Y3, Canada
[a division of Pearson Penguin Canada Inc.]
Penguin Books Ltd
80 Strand, London WC2R 0RL, England
Penguin Ireland
25 St Stephen's Green, Dublin 2, Ireland
[a division of Penguin Books Ltd]
Penguin Books India Pvt Ltd
11 Community Centre, Panchsheel Park, New Delhi – 110 017, India
Penguin Group [NZ]
Cnr Airborne and Rosedale Roads, Albany, Auckland, New Zealand
[a division of Pearson New Zealand Ltd]
Penguin Books [South Africa] [Pty] Ltd
24 Sturdee Avenue, Rosebank, Johannesburg 2196, South Africa

Penguin Books Ltd, Registered Offices: 80 Strand, London, WC2R 0RL, England

First published by Penguin Group [Australia], a division of Pearson Australia Group Pty Ltd, 2010

10 9 8 7 6 5 4 3 2 1

Text copyright © Damien Pignolet 2010
Photographs copyright © Anson Smart 2010

The moral right of the author has been asserted

All rights reserved. Without limiting the rights under copyright reserved above, no part of this
publication may be reproduced, stored in or introduced into a retrieval system, or transmitted, in
any form or by any means [electronic, mechanical, photocopying, recording or otherwise], without
the prior written permission of both the copyright owner and the above publisher of this book.

Design by emeryfrost © Penguin Group [Australia]
Design coordination by Evi O.
Photography by Anson Smart
Prop styling by Margot Braddon
Cover illustration by Michael Fitzjames
Typeset in Tribute by Post Pre-press Group, Brisbane, Queensland
Colour reproduction by Splitting Image, Clayton, Victoria
Printed and bound in China by 1010 Printing International Limited

National Library of Australia
Cataloguing-in-Publication data:

Pignolet, Damien.
Salades / Damien Pignolet.

9781920989552 (hbk.)
Includes index.
Bibliography.

Salads.
Cookery, French.

641.83

penguin.com.au